# ARNIETEX

OVER 100 RECIPES FOR MEXICAN-AMERICAN COOKING AND TEXAS-STYLE BBQ

# ARNIETEX

OVER 100 RECIPES FOR MEXICAN-AMERICAN COOKING AND TEXAS-STYLE BBQ

## ARNIE SEGOVIA

**Publisher** Mike Sanders
**Art & Design Director** William Thomas
**Editorial Director** Ann Barton
**Senior Editor** Brook Farling
**Senior Designer** Rebecca Batchelor
**Developmental Editor** Christy Wagner
**Food Stylist and Art Director** Ivanna Mendoza
**Food Photographer** Ismael Martinez
**Culinary Assistants** Meira Eustaquio, Frida Salinas
**Lifestyle and Cover Photographer** Eli Infante
**Proofreaders** Jean Bissell, Monica Stone
**Indexer** Beverlee Day

First American Edition, 2025
Published in the United States by DK Publishing
1745 Broadway, 20th Floor, New York, NY 10019

The authorized representative in the EEA is Dorling Kindersley
Verlag GmbH. Arnulfstr. 124, 80636 Munich, Germany

Copyright © Arnie Segovia
DK, a Division of Penguin Random House LLC
25 26 27 28 29    10 9 8 7 6 5 4
004–344494–JUL2025

A catalog record for this book
is available from the Library of Congress.
ISBN 978-0-5939-5864-3

DK books are available at special discounts when purchased
in bulk for sales promotions, premiums, fund-raising, or
educational use. For details, contact SpecialSales@dk.com

Printed and bound in Latvia

**www.dk.com**

MIX
Paper | Supporting
responsible forestry
FSC™ C018179

This book was made with Forest
Stewardship Council™ certified
paper – one small step in DK's
commitment to a sustainable future.
Learn more at
www.dk.com/uk/information/sustainability

This book is dedicated to my parents, Josefina Segovia, aka "MommaTex," and Arnulfo Segovia Jr. I'd also like to dedicate this book to my maternal grandparents, Esmeralda "Lala" & Jose Rosales, as well as to my paternal grandmother, Leandra Segovia, all of whom have given me memories and inspiration I will cherish forever.

# CONTENTS

★ ★ ★

Introduction ..................................... 7

## 1 ¡VÁMONOS! ................... 11

The Journey ................................. 12
Tools ............................................ 16
Grills and Smokers ....................... 20
Flavor .......................................... 24
Philosophy and Pro Tips .............. 28

## 2 SALSAS, SAUCES, AND MARINADES ................. 33

Pico de Gallo ................................ 34
Salsa Roja–Ranchera .................... 37
Salsa Roja–Boiled ........................ 38
Salsa Roja–Taqueria ..................... 39
Salsa Verde–Base ......................... 40
Salsa Verde–Tomatillos ................ 42
Salsa Verde–Taqueria ................... 43
Salsa Verde–Aguacate .................. 44
Salsa Taquera .............................. 45
Creamy Habanero Salsa ............... 47
Fire-Roasted Salsa ....................... 48
Salsa Chipotle en Adobo .............. 50
Salsa Chile Piquín ........................ 51
Salsa Puya ................................... 52
Salsa Macha ................................. 55
Chile Guajillo Sauce ..................... 56
Al Pastor Adobo ........................... 59
Red Carniceria Marinade .............. 60
Green Fajita Marinade .................. 62
Chile Toreados ............................. 63

Salsa Tatemada ............................ 64
Salsa Tuétano .............................. 65

## 3 BREAKFAST ................... 67

Con Huevos–Papas ....................... 68
Con Huevos–Bacon ...................... 70
Con Huevos–Chorizo ..................... 71
Con Huevos–Nopales .................... 72
Barbacoa Especial ....................... 73
Choripapas ................................... 74
Chicharrón en Salsa Verde ........... 77
Chilaquiles Rojos .......................... 78
Migas .......................................... 81
Machacado à la Mexicana ............. 82
Huevos Rancheros ........................ 85
Huevos Divorciados ...................... 86
Costra de Queso ........................... 89

## 4 TAQUERIA EL ARNIE ......... 91

Easy al Pastor Tacos ..................... 92
Gringas ........................................ 93
Crispy Tacos ................................ 94
Baja Fish and Shrimp Tacos .......... 95
Tortas de Deshebrada ................... 96
Tacos Gobernador ......................... 99
Cacheteadas ................................ 100
Tacos de Bistec ........................... 103

## 5 FAJITA FEST ................. 105

Fajitas–Skirt Steak ...................... 107
Fajitas–Restaurant Style .............. 108
Chicken Fajitas ............................ 111

## 6 ARNIE'S CAFÉ AND GRILL .. 113

ArnieTex Tejano Burger ................ 115
Hamburgesa Mexicana ................. 116
Steak (Porterhouse or T-Bone) ...... 119
Steak (Rib Eye) ............................ 121
Carne Guisada ............................. 122
Asado de Puerco .......................... 125
Botana (RGV Style) ....................... 126

Sombrero Plate .......................129
Steak Ranchero ......................130
Tostadas (aka Chalupas)....................133
Carne con Papas....................134
Caldo de Pollo ......................135
Arroz con Pollo.....................136
Calabaza con Pollo .................139
Chile Colorado ......................140
Flautas................................143
Picadillo ..............................144
Enchiladas Rojas...................145
Enchiladas Suizas .................146
Texas Chili Enchiladas ..........149
Tex-Mex Enchiladas ............. 150
Caldo de Res........................153
Ceviche ..............................154
Pollo Guisado.......................155

## 7 MI RANCHITO ................. 157

Discada Norteña....................159
Texas Chili ........................... 160
Menudo ...............................163
Parrillada .............................164
Dove Poppers.......................166
Fideo ...................................167
Smoked Barbacoa .................169
Birria de Res.........................170
Mollejas ..............................173
Carnitas...............................174
Pan de Campo .....................177
Tamales ...............................178

## 8 TEJANO BAR-B-QUE ....... 181

Pulled Pork...........................183
Texas Brisket ........................184
Texas Pork Ribs (Arnie Style) ...............187
Pork Belly Chicharrón ........... 188
Smoked Turkey Breast ......... 190
Grilled Chicken Thighs (Two Ways)....191
Grilled Chicken Leg Quarters.............192
Texas Chicken Halves ...........195
Beef Ribs (Finger Ribs)..........196
Beef Ribs (Monster Ribs) .......198
Beef Ribs (Loaded Ribs) ........199

## 9 LOS SIDES ..................... 201

Charro Beans........................202
Basic Beans–Traditional.....................204
Refried Beans–Three Ways ...............205
MommaTex's Mexican Rice ...............207
Guacamole ......................... 208
Quick Pickled Onions ......... 210
Totopos ...............................211
Choriqueso ..........................213
Papa Asada ..........................214
Potato Salad .........................215

Acknowledgments ................217
Index....................................218
About the Author....................224

# INTRODUCTION

★ ★ ★

I was born in Phoenix, Arizona, but have lived most of my life in Texas, surrounded by family and friends, making memories together. The best memories often come from getting together to cook with family, watching Mom, Dad, uncles, and grandparents work their magic in the kitchen or over the grill. It's in these moments, full of laughter and good food, that traditions are born and cherished.

This book isn't just a collection of recipes; it's a story of love, family, and all the good things that come from gathering around a fire or in a kitchen to share food. It's also a journey through my life and my own personal culinary development, which has brought me so much passion and meaning. I hope you feel that same joy with every recipe, and I thank you for letting me be a part of your culinary journey.

I've poured my heart and soul into this book, and I hope you love the recipes. But cooking isn't just about following the instructions. Yes, cooking amazing food is about finding the right balance of flavor, texture, and experience, but great food also comes from love, passion, and, most importantly, preference. It's impossible for every recipe to be "perfect" for everyone. So as you work through this book, I encourage you to experiment with the recipes, to tweak, test, fine-tune, and make them truly your own!

¡Vámonos!

Arnie

# 1

# ¡VÁMONOS!

# THE JOURNEY

★ ★ ★

## FARM AND RANCH LIFE

I was born in Phoenix, Arizona, but I crawled to Texas as fast as I could.

My parents, both from South Texas, followed friends to Arizona in search of new opportunities. But within a year, they returned to Texas, setting down roots on a 7,000-acre farm and ranch in West Texas, between Pecos and Balmorhea. My dad was the foreman there, and I grew up surrounded by cotton fields, tumbleweeds, and oil rigs. We were about 30 miles away from the nearest town.

I spent weekends and summers riding my bike to the local co-op coffee shop, sipping free coffee and listening to farmers share stories about their crops and their lives. Sometimes I'd stop by the cotton gin, buy a Coke, and drop peanuts into the bottle—now, that was a treat. Life on the farm was rich with experiences, from my first tastes of cabrito and chicharrónes to helping harvest and cook a whole cow over a weekend. The fires burned, the beer flowed, and music filled the nights until early Monday mornings.

Jeff, the owner's son, became my best friend. Together, we had the kind of adventures kids dream of, like trekking to the landfill to shoot lizards with our BB guns or cooking weenies and canned food over open campfires. Watching my dad and neighbors cook over fires and having my own campfire adventures with Jeff sparked my fascination with fire and cooking.

At a young age, I worked the cotton rows, chopping weeds with my mom and our neighbors. I can still taste the homemade tacos the ladies prepared for lunch and the sweet, cold slices of fresh-picked watermelon in the afternoon. By the time I was 11, I was driving tractors. The men nicknamed my tractor the "ghost tractor" because I was so small it looked like it was driving itself.

Those days were incredible, filled with moments that you only truly appreciate years later as an adult.

## SOUTH TEXAS

In the mid-1970s, we moved back to South Texas, and my parents bought a small, 5-acre property we called "The Ranch." It quickly became the family gathering place for music, food, fire, and fun. The men made barbacoa de cabeza overnight in a pit in the ground, and we feasted like kings the next morning. The women kept the fires going, boiling tomatoes to can or making delicious comida casera like carne guisada, asado de puerco, tamales, arroz, frijoles, salsas, tortillas a mano, and pico de gallo. Just like in West Texas, these gatherings lasted all weekend.

When Terry and I got married, my Tío Rudy gifted us a small barbecue grill. That's when I started grilling my own fajitas, chicken, and sausage, although I still loved cooking in the kitchen, too. During our second year of marriage, Terry and I even went vegetarian for a few years, and I grilled oatmeal burgers and veggie dishes for church potlucks. I know, I know—ArnieTex, a vegetarian? But trust me, my friends were always amazed at how good the food I cooked tasted. I started to learn then that cooking was one of my God-given gifts.

I spent a few years working at a local sugar mill, and eventually found myself selling cars—a perfect fit for a car-loving "gearhead" like me. Soon I was making big sales, and as I worked my way up to be the manager of a large dealership, I often grilled and smoked meats for my team's lunch 6 days a week. We were fortunate to have bosses who allowed us to enjoy barbecue on the job. This routine—or rather ritual—helped me refine my grilling and barbecue skills.

I entered my first barbecue competition in 1998 and discovered that I had a real knack for it. My brother and I built my first trailer pit, The Smokin' Lonestar, and my boss agreed to let me take one Saturday off each month to compete. Terry and I bought an RV and hit the road for cook-offs, winning plenty of trophies along the way. We took a break from competing for a few years to focus on dirt bike racing with the kids, often bringing our grill to the local track to cook for everyone there.

During my dealership years, I'd cook briskets for friends in a brick barbecue pit I built in my backyard. It was a 42 × 96-inch (1 × 2.5m) pit with two large flat lids, just like the big restaurant pits, able to hold 20 briskets at a time. I was practically living on barbecue back then, cooking every day of the week.

I eventually left the car business and bought a Mexican restaurant in San Juan, Texas. The 2008 financial crash hit us hard, however, and we eventually sold it. Still, I loved the restaurant business and cherished the smiles and conversations with our Arnie's Café & Grill customers for the years we were in business.

It was at the restaurant that I developed a deep respect for authentic Mexican food and true Tex-Mex cuisine, learning from talented chefs who taught me what real flavors were about. Even today, it's hard to find a Mexican restaurant that can live up to the food we served at ours. Many of the recipes in this book are my best attempt to capture and share the spirit and flavor of those recipes.

# A RETURN ᴛᴏ COMPETITIONS, PLUS CLASSES ᴀɴᴅ CONTENT

After the kids left for college, Terry and I returned to barbecue competitions, hitting our stride in 2013 and quickly becoming one of the winningest barbecue teams in Texas. It was then that I really learned that competition barbecue demands intense, one-bite "flavor bombs" loaded with injections, brines, and additives—basically, anything you can do to win. This was a stark contrast from how I cooked at home, where I kept things simple with foods cooked slowly and gently, with love and care.

In 2017, I was inducted into the International Barbeque Cookers Association Hall of Fame—a proud moment, and an honor I shared that year with one of my heroes, Ronnie Wade, who is the winningest barbecue competitor in Texas history.

It was around this time that my son, Dan, and I launched the "ArnieTex" brand on social media. It was a wild hair of an idea Dan proposed—I didn't fully understand what it could be at the time—but we started documenting my day-to-day life and posted the videos on YouTube.

I started teaching other teams my methods in 2016, and that eventually led to the creation of my online Pitmaster Class in 2019, during which I shared my most detailed backyard and competition recipes. Since then, I've been honored to host these classes for more than 3,200 students, with my Brisket Masterclass being the bestseller. The process of recording, editing, and releasing the classes was a monumental effort that completely pulled me away from the competition trail, and it would be a sign of things to come. Once the classes were live, we needed a way to market them, so we kept chugging along on YouTube, recording and sharing videos when we could.

Then came the global pandemic, which shut down everything. In-person classes were completely off the table, and the organic interest in my online classes had evened out. Then one day an email arrived from a huge tech company, which was partnered with another huge tech company, that asked if I could host 3 days of barbecue demos live and online for their corporate partners.

We scrambled to put together a live production for 3 days, and it went off without a hitch. The partners loved it, and most importantly, we made some good money—enough to invest in finally launching my barbecue and carne asada rubs. I can remember timidly placing the order and paying for the 1,500 shakers of rubs, worried that we wouldn't be able to sell them. Much to my surprise, we sold out in 4 days! The content, recipes, and value we had been providing for the past three years had built up so much goodwill with my audience. I was finally starting to understand this crazy life of content creation. I immediately ordered 20,000 more shakers.

The rest, as they say, is history. My family and I would triple-down on social media, releasing a few hundred YouTube videos and thousands of short-form pieces of content, all of which led to this book being published and you holding it in your hands right now.

Sometimes I zoom out and look at everything that has happened in the past few years and think "Wow." Never in my wildest dreams could I have imagined having a career as a "content creator." It's one that didn't exist in my grandparents' generation, yet many of the recipes in this book have been influenced by or have a direct connection to them because they handed them down to my parents, who handed them down to me, and now I'm proud to be able to share them with you.

¡Vámonos!

# TOOLS

★ ★ ★

Barbecue is a relatively simple method of cooking. It's mostly two things, time and love, that produce great barbecue. Still, some tools do make the process easier.

## BARBECUE TOOLS

An infinite number of specialty barbecue tools are available, but here are the ones I use and believe are most important:

**A 6-INCH (15CM) BONING KNIFE (1)** is helpful for trimming meat; it's light and easy to maneuver; and it has a sharp pointed tip to get under the silverskin and membrane on some cuts.

**AN 8-INCH (20CM) FILET KNIFE (2)** is excellent for filleting fish, trimming delicate meat, and getting under silverskin and membranes with finesse.

**AN 8-INCH (20CM) BREAKING KNIFE (3)** is basically a bigger, heavier version of a boning knife. I use this for most trimming.

**AN 8-INCH (20CM) CHEF KNIFE (4)** is the most indispensable knife. It can do it all if necessary, and it's my go-to choice for slicing meats other than big briskets or turkeys, but it could easily do that, too.

**A 10-INCH (25.5CM) SLICER (5)** is my favorite knife for slicing big cuts like brisket into nice, clean, straight slices.

**GLOVES (6)**  High-heat gloves are an essential safety tool for grilling. Handling hot grates, smokers, or equipment without proper protection can cause serious burns. Find a quality brand and pair that fits your hands and that you're comfortable with. I prefer silicone gloves or some welding gloves that can be discarded after many uses. Burns are no joke!

**LARGE ICE SCOOP (7)**  This is handy for scooping charcoal into your grill or smoker in smaller amounts.

**SAUCEPANS**  Good pans are helpful on the grill as well as in the kitchen (more on that coming up). I use small stainless-steel saucepans on the barbecue for melting butter, warming sauces, basting, and so much more.

**ASH SCRAPER (8)**  This tool is readily available at big-box stores and is helpful for rearranging your fire and coals. It's also a good tool to scrape out the ash from previous cooks.

**TONGS (9)**  I use heavy-duty restaurant-style tongs available at restaurant supply stores. I've tried many different types and designs, but the restaurant-style tongs are sturdy and will last for years. They come in various lengths and will stand up to lots of use and abuse. I have several pairs of tongs in each size; long and extra-large ones are great for grilling over fire and provide more leverage and control.

**BASTING BRUSHES (10)**  Basting brushes are used to coat barbecue sauce or butter onto meat. I like silicone brushes.

**SCISSORS/SHEARS (11)**  These are great for finer trimming of meats as well as various other uses, such as spatchcocking chicken. Invest in a good pair.

**SERVING SPOONS (12)**  Stainless-steel serving spoons, both with and without holes, are a must. They last forever and are sanitary.

**SKEWERS (13)**  Skewers are helpful when grilling various cuts and meats over fire, for kabobs, and for roasting salsa ingredients, such as tomatoes, onions, and peppers. I recommend stainless steel.

**SPIDER STRAINER (14)**  I often use a spider strainer to hold and toast smaller chiles directly over coals. (These also are helpful in the kitchen; more on that coming up.)

**DIGITAL MEAT THERMOMETER (15)**  Get a good-quality digital meat thermometer to check the internal temperature of your meat. These come in various shapes, sizes, and quality.

**INFRARED THERMOMETER (16)**  I also recommend an infrared laser thermometer. These are great for checking the surface temperature of cooking grates, griddles, and pans when you need a consistent, high grate temperature for sear marks.

# KITCHEN TOOLS

In addition to a great set of basics like bowls and utensils, here's what I use on a regular basis in the kitchen:

**BLENDER**   A good-quality commercial-grade blender can make all the difference when blending salsas and especially adobos. When blending dried chiles, it's important to have a blender that can chop them to a fine consistency for maximum volume and flavor. I own three and recommend blenders with glass containers.

**CANNING JARS**   I use glass to store food almost exclusively. I don't like to store food, especially hot food, in plastic, although sometimes it's necessary. For any salsas, adobos, or marinades, it's always glass for me. I keep a stock of several sizes of canning jars in my pantry, including 1 cup, 2½ cups, and 3 cups.

**COMALS/GRIDDLES**   Comals, or griddles, come in many different sizes and shapes, and although you can cook and heat tortillas in a pan, a comal works so much better due to the quality and thickness of the metal. Mine stays on the stovetop 24/7.

**COUNTERTOP OVEN**   This is an optional-but-nice-to-have item. I love mine for smaller cooking, like Pork Belly Chicharrón (page 188), baking chickens, and reheating leftovers. Yes, I eat lots of leftovers! Many brands make these ovens, so find one that's good quality and fits your budget and space.

**CUTTING BOARDS**   I always use wooden cutting boards, and I have a collection of several sizes, weights, and finishes. Wooden boards are great and require little maintenance. I'm not a fan of plastic cutting boards; tiny, micro-slivers of the board can break off with use.

**FOOD/PREP TRAYS**   These are versatile pieces of kitchen equipment, handy for corralling ingredients, seasoning meat and vegetables in large quantities, and more.

**FUNNELS**   I use various sizes and diameters of funnels for pouring salsas, broths, marinades, brines, etc. They also are useful when pouring seasoning blends into shakers.

**MEASURING CUPS AND SPOONS (19)**
I recommend stainless-steel measuring cups and spoons. Buy a good-quality brand. It's worth it because they will ensure that your measurements are consistent all the time.

Some cheaper-quality versions don't measure as precisely as a solid set will.

**MEAT GRINDER**   I got by for many years with a grinder attachment on my stand mixer, and that's probably okay for the typical home cook. I grind a lot of meat for sausage and burgers, so I upgraded to a commercial grinder. Look for a smaller one that fits your budget and needs.

**MOLCAJETE**   A molcajete is basically an old-school mortar and pestle used by many home cooks in Mexican culture and cuisine. I like to collect these, so I have several, but my favorite is the one my grandmother used on a daily basis. It's probably 75 to 80 years old, and it's magical. These are used only for grinding spices or mashing salsa ingredients.

**NONSTICK SKILLETS**   Skillets serve a variety of uses in the kitchen, from frying to sautéing. I recommend having a few sizes of nonstick skillets, such as 8 inches (20cm), 10 inches (25.5cm), and 12 inches (30.5cm).

**SPICE GRINDER**   A spice grinder is simply a good-quality coffee grinder that is dedicated to blending or grinding only spices.

**SPOONS AND SPATULAS**   I love cooking with stainless-steel and wooden spoons rather than with plastic or metal. Wooden spoons have a gentler feel to them when sautéing or stirring guisados or other delicate foods. Wood is also easier on the surface of your pans, so they'll last longer, too. High-heat silicone spatulas have a time and place. I only use them when cooking in nonstick pans, especially when preparing eggs.

**STAINLESS-STEEL SKILLETS, SAUCEPANS, AND SAUCIER PANS**   Having a range of these pans will enable you to cook just about everything, from vegetables to sauces and adobos. I suggest having them in 8-inch (20cm), 10-inch (25.5cm), and 12-inch (30.5cm) sizes.

**STRAINERS AND SIEVES (17)**   I use fine-mesh strainers when making large-volume sauces and adobos. A stainless-steel conical strainer is a really useful tool and is available in various mesh sizes. I use both. These are also known as a bouillon strainer or chinois and are available in different sizes. Spider strainers are helpful when frying or straining ingredients.

**TONGS (18)**   In addition to the long and extra-long tongs used for grilling and mentioned earlier, I use small and medium tongs while cooking in the kitchen and for serving. I also have several small tongs with silicone tips that I use with nonstick pans.

# GRILLS AND SMOKERS

★ ★ ★

You have many options when cooking over fire: grilling, smoking, carne asada, and more, and there are just as many different types of grills and smokers to get the job done. Take into consideration your budget, backyard space, cooking preferences, and goals when choosing the grill or smoker, and accompanying fuel, that's right for you. You can barbecue over any type of flame, from open fire to the most complicated of grill setups. Here are some types of grills and smokers I've used.

**DRUM SMOKERS (1)**   Drum smokers have a vertical design to maximize cooking space on the 22-inch (56cm) drum for large cuts of meat like brisket, butts, and ribs. Drums are popular on the competition circuit, where they're endearingly called "ugly drum smokers." Inexpensive and lightweight, drums take up little space, are great for grilling and smoking, and can cook for 12 to 20 hours on a single load of fuel. The downside is they that can't cook a lot of meat at one time and are not the best for direct grilling.

**KETTLES (2)**   The popular Weber Kettle is widely regarded as one of the best, due to its versatility, affordability, and durable construction. Its simple yet effective design allows for direct and indirect grilling. You can sear steaks and burgers as well as cook larger cuts like whole briskets, butts, and chickens. The porcelain-enameled body is rust resistant and retains heat well. Accessories and add-ons make it a great value.

**OPEN-FIRE GRILLS (3)**   Open-fire grills have become a sensation due to the primal, rustic grilling experience and the unique, smoky flavor they impart. Flames directly beneath allow for high-heat searing and development of a rich char that's hard to replicate with other grilling methods. Open-fire grills are tricky and take practice. Getting the fire right is important, especially in the smaller ones. Larger open-fire cookers require constant attention and fuel, especially on windy days. You'll have to consider the amount of wood it takes to cook on them regularly if you're thinking of buying a bigger open-fire grill; wood storage, capacity, and a local supplier are essential. It takes work to cook on these grills, but if you love playing with fire like I do, then it's just plain fun. One downside is that they rust quickly if not cared for properly.

**PELLET GRILLS AND SMOKERS (4)**   I might have been one of the first barbecuers in Texas to own a pellet grill, way back in 1998. These grills have come a long way since then, thanks to modern technology. They cook with real wood pellets compressed under high pressure, starting, stopping, and maintaining a certain fan speed that feeds pellets to maintain the temperature set. They can cook low and slow, at 175°F (80°C) to 180°F (83°C), or hot and fast, at 700°F (370°C) in some models. Pellet grills are amazing during the hot summer months when it's 115°F (46°C) outside—just set it, forget it, and enjoy the delicious results.

**PORTABLE GRILLS (5)**   Portable grills are ideal for grilling and smoking while tailgating, camping, RVing, or traveling. My favorite is the NOMAD, from Dallas, Texas. Rugged and portable, it combines heavy-duty Texas-style barbecue with modern, minimalist design. The rust-resistant cast-aluminum body is lightweight and durable, offers good heat retention, folds like a suitcase, and has an optional grate for cooking on both sides or a griddle as pictured. Many brands, sizes, and shapes of portable grills are sold to fit any budget.

**SANTA MARIA GRILLS (6)**   The Santa Maria–style grill is fast becoming the most popular grill in the country. With roots in Santa Maria, a city in Santa Barbara County on California's Central Coast, this style of grilling became popular in the mid-nineteenth century among ranchers who used it to cook for large gatherings and celebrations, particularly "barbecues" after cattle roundups. The setup includes a metal grill grate raised or lowered over the fire to control the cooking temperature— the key feature that distinguishes it from other barbecue methods. The Santa Maria grill, with its flavorful approach to open-fire cooking, has become iconic in American barbecue culture.

**SPINNING ASADO CROSSES (7)**   In northern Mexico, cabrito (young goat) is traditionally cooked over open flames or hot coals in a style known as cabrito al pastor. This method involves slow-roasting the goat on a spit or metal rack, called an asado cross, over mesquite wood for

a delicious, smoky flavor. An asado cross is a traditional metal framework used to grill large cuts of meat, particularly whole animals like lamb, goat, or whole hogs. The asado cross has a dramatic presentation and is a central part of northern Mexican and South American barbecue culture, where it's a popular technique for gatherings and special occasions. Leave it to a Texan to make something great even better! Pictured is the Spinning Asado Cross by Big Jav's BBQ, which can spin and rotate 360 degrees while lowering the animal close and far from the fire. Some are even fabricated to cook whole cows.

**TEXAS PIPE SMOKERS AND GRILLS (8)** These have become all of the rage in recent years, especially for barbecue restaurants. Texas-style pipe and propane-tank smokers and grills are heavy-duty smokers crafted from repurposed oil pipes, made from heavy-duty ¼-inch (0.5cm) steel, and are able to handle long slow-cooked barbecue for authentic Texas-style brisket, ribs, and more. These smokers use offset fireboxes to keep the heat and smoke separate from the main cooking chamber; utilize "sticks" (or logs) for indirect cooking that results in tender, smoky meat; and retain heat, efficiently maintaining steady temperatures for hours. They do require constant attention to maintain ideal temperatures and they're large, heavy, and take up a lot of space for the smoker and the wood storage. But Texas-style barbecue, when done right on a stick burner, creates a wonderful flavor. These smokers will last for years with proper care and maintenance.

**TEXAS TRAILER SMOKERS (9)** Texas trailer smokers are mobile, with a large cooking capacity and a rugged design tailored for the Texas barbecue scene. These are the standard in Texas barbecue competitions. These smokers are high quality, with thick steel that retains heat over extended cook times, and are often equipped with large, offset fireboxes that ensure even, indirect heat for low-and-slow smoking. Size and design allow for cooking large quantities for gatherings, events, and barbecue competitions. Many Texas trailer smokers are custom made, featuring adjustable vents, multilevel grates, and additional features like warming racks or vertical smoking chambers. They're popular with pitmasters who need versatility and the ability to serve barbecue on the road.

**OUTDOOR GRIDDLES (10)** Outdoor griddles (or planchas in Spanish) are flat, wide cooking surfaces designed for cooking everything from pancakes to burgers. Their fuel sources are propane or electricity. They come in various sizes and are great for cooking for families or large groups.

**¡VÁMONOS!** 21

# FIRE STARTERS

Get fired up! I have used many fire-starter methods during the years, depending what cooker I'm using, as well as how much fuel is required.

**CHARCOAL CHIMNEYS**  Charcoal chimneys are a metal cylinder with a grate near the bottom that holds charcoal while airflow ignites the coals. I use a tumbleweed starter underneath to light them. In about 15 to 20 minutes, the coals will be ready to be poured into the grill. Chimneys are popular, fast, consistent, and don't require lighter fluid.

**LIGHTER FLUID**  Traditional lighter fluid is sprayed onto charcoal and ignited. It's quick to use and readily available, but it does have drawbacks, like the potential for a chemical taste on meat if not used correctly. I always wait until the charcoal is fully lit and gray before cooking on a fire lit with lighter fluid. I rarely use lighter fluid, but I always keep some handy, just in case.

**LONG LIGHTERS (1)**  The go-to method of lighting fires, whether at the grill or in the home, long lighters are easy to use, inexpensive, and refillable. I have a collection in various sizes.

**PEAR BURNERS & MINI LOG LIGHTERS (2)**  Pear burners are big torches used to light logs quickly so you can start cooking sooner. Originally, they were used for burning thorns off cacti, allowing cattle to feed on the delicious, nutritious, high-water-content cactus. Pear burners come in various lengths and designs, and some are made specifically for barbecue. Mini log lighters, which are my favorite, are light, easy to use, and powerful.

**TUMBLEWEEDS (3)**  Tumbleweed fire starters have become very popular in recent years. These natural fire starters are made of compressed wood fibers covered in wax and designed to help ignite charcoal, wood, and other barbecue fuels quickly and easily.

# FUEL

Finding your preferred fuel for barbecue and grilling is a process that takes time, experimentation, and lots of trial and error, but eventually you will find what works best for you. There are a lot of different fuels, each with its own flavor, pros, and cons. Master all of them and you will always be prepared for grilling on anything, at any time.

**CHARCOAL BRIQUETTES (4)**   Charcoal briquettes are made of compressed saw dust and coal with additives that ensure a consistent burn time and temperature. A high-quality brand of charcoal has more coal uniformity and burns longer and hotter with more consistency; others may contain more dust and burn out quicker.

**LUMP CHARCOAL (5)**   Lump charcoal is made from pure hardwood, burns hotter than briquettes, and imparts a more natural, smoky flavor. It is also more responsive to airflow and gives you finer control over the heat.

**HARDWOOD LOGS (6)**   Used in traditional offset smokers or open-pit barbecues, hardwood logs create rich, authentic, smoky flavors and are ideal for low-and-slow cooking. Popular woods include hickory, oak, pecan, mesquite, and fruitwoods, like apple and cherry. Each brings its own unique flavor profile.

**NATURAL WOOD SPLITS (7)**   Burning wood splits (mini logs) to embers before cooking is a popular method used in open-fire cooking and Santa Maria–style barbecue. It combines wood and charcoal qualities to create a subtle, distinct flavor.

**PELLETS (8)**   Pellets are compressed sawdust formed into small, uniform pellets used primarily in pellet smokers. These are convenient and offer consistent heat and flavor with various wood options (hickory, apple, mesquite, etc.). They work well for set-and-forget styles of barbecue, especially on hot summer days or cold winter days. They also are often used like wood chips in charcoal fires.

**WOOD CHIPS (9)**   Wood chips are added to charcoal fires for an extra smoky boost. Chips provide quick bursts of smoke without adding a full log.

**WOOD CHUNKS (10)**   Like wood chips, wood chunks are added to charcoal fires for an extra smoky boost. Chunks offer a longer, steadier smoke than chips. Various wood types allow barbecuers to layer in flavors with chips and chunks, without using a full log. They're particularly useful for smaller cookers.

# WOOD SPECIES AND FLAVOR PROFILES

You can use several types of wood when grilling and smoking meats. Many people cook with what's local to their area, but you can pick up a variety of flavors of wood or pellets at most big-box stores. Each has unique flavors and smoking properties, enabling you to experiment with combinations to enhance different types of meat.

**APPLE**   Applewood has a mild, slightly sweet, and fruity flavor. It's great with pork, poultry, and seafood.

**HICKORY**   Hickory has a strong, smoky, and slightly sweet flavor with bacon-like undertones. It's nice for any meat but especially pork. I once smoked some monster beef ribs with hickory, and some friends thought the ribs came from a huge pig because they tasted like bacon.

**MESQUITE**   Mesquite can be strong and intense, earthy and robust, with a distinct Texas aroma and flavor. It burns hotter and longer than any other wood and requires more air to burn clean for smoking—the secret is to have translucent exhaust rather than thin blue or gray smoke. Some people think mesquite is too strong, but when used correctly, it can create wonderfully flavored barbecue. It's hard to beat when grilling steaks, fajitas, chops, burgers, or chicken. When smoking brisket, I prefer a blend of mesquite and post oak or mesquite and pecan.

**PECAN**   Pecan is a cousin to hickory. It is rich, nutty, and slightly sweet, and it puts a pretty red color on meat. A favorite on the competition trail, pecan is mild with a great flavor profile that judges love. It's versatile, blends well with other woods, and is great for grilling all meats and seafood.

**POST OAK**   This is the most famous and preferred wood in Texas barbecue. Post oak is a medium-smoky, slightly nutty wood that's milder than hickory but stronger than fruit woods. It makes long-lasting coals, burns steadily and evenly, and offers a balanced flavor that compliments most meats. It's also a great choice for grilling your favorite meats.

# FLAVOR

★ ★ ★

When I was competing on the barbecue trail, two important things I tried to give the judges were tenderness and flavor. Flavor is what makes you go "Yum" and "Ooooh, that's good" and "More, please." You achieve flavor in part via the cooking method but also by using a variety of seasonings, sauces, marinades, and more.

## SPICES, HERBS, AND OTHER SEASONINGS

Different regions, countries, and cultures all have their own set of daily spices—what I call the "familiar flavor." Mexican and South American cuisines are rich in spices to create distinct, layered flavors. Here are some key spices, herbs, and other seasonings commonly used to bring the bold, complex flavors that define northern Mexican and Tex-Mex cuisine:

**ACHIOTE**  Achiote, or annatto, adds mild, peppery notes and a vibrant red color to dishes. It's used in Mexican and Central American cooking to add color to rice and meats.

**BAY LEAVES**  Bay leaves have a subtle, woodsy flavor that compliments slow-cooked meats and beans, helping balance richer flavors. They're added to broths, stews, and sauces in Mexican and Tex-Mex cooking.

**BLACK PEPPER**  Black pepper is a pungent, slightly spicy spice with a sharp, earthy flavor. It's highly versatile and used to season both savory and sweet dishes. Black pepper enhances meats, vegetables, soups, and sauces; is used in rubs; and acts as a finishing touch, often with salt, to elevate the natural flavors of food. Freshly ground black pepper offers the most robust flavor. If you could only have two ingredients to cook with in your kitchen, this should be one of them, with the other being salt.

**CINNAMON**  Mexican cinnamon, or canela, is softer and more floral than the cassia cinnamon commonly sold in the United States. It's used in both sweet dishes, like arroz con leche, and savory dishes, like moles and adobos.

**CILANTRO**  Cilantro is a fresh herb used in many Mexican dishes, including salsas, guacamole, tacos, and soups. The fresh leaves and stems are commonly used to add brightness to dishes.

**CLOVE**  This warm, aromatic spice is used in Mexican and South American cooking, in dishes such as moles and stews, to add depth and complexity.

**CUMIN**  Cumin seeds, whole or ground, are a cornerstone in Mexican and Tex-Mex dishes. Cumin adds a warm, earthy, spicy depth to dishes like chili, beans, barbacoa, moles, and meat rubs and other seasonings, as well as many South American marinades and sauces.

**OREGANO**  Mexican oregano has a robust, citrusy, and anise-like flavor compared to Mediterranean oregano. It's added to salsas, stews, and soups for a deeper, earthy flavor.

**PAPRIKA**  Paprika is made from dried chile peppers, red peppers, sweet peppers, jalapeños, cayennes, or bell peppers. It is used in many South American and southwestern United States dishes.

**SALT**  Salt is an essential seasoning. When used early in the cooking process, salt allows flavors to meld, and more can be added later, if needed, to further enhance the taste of the finished dish. I use different salts at various stages; I use coarse kosher salt for large meats like brisket, for example, and flaked sea salt as my go-to for seasoning for just about everything else and for dusting steaks and fajitas during the rest period.

Some salts taste slightly different, some contain additives, some are stronger, and some are lighter in weight and, therefore, less salty when applied—1 tablespoon of coarse kosher salt does not weigh the same as 1 tablespoon of fine sea salt. The best way to substitute salts is to weigh them.

I recommend experimenting with salts as you cook to find your preferred flavors, textures, and overall saltiness threshold. Here are a few to try:

- *Coarse kosher salt* is ideal on big meats like briskets and pork butts for barbecue. Coarse kosher's flake-like structure makes it easy to pinch and sprinkle during cooking, although I prefer a shaker for more even distribution. Kosher salt dissolves quickly and has no additives, giving it a purer flavor.

- *Diamond kosher salt* has a unique, flaky texture and is lighter than other kosher salts. It dissolves quickly in food and cooking applications, making it versatile for seasoning and brining.

- *Sea salt* is my favorite everyday salt, and I always have a few different versions and brands on hand. It is made from evaporated seawater and retains its natural minerals, which can give it a complex flavor. It's often used as a finishing salt to add a subtle crunch and a hint of briny flavor. Sea salt can be found in fine grains, which work well in general cooking.

- *Table salt* is fine for most recipes in this book, and I recommend Morton's non-iodized table salt, unless a recipe specifies otherwise. Refined, fine-grained salt is iodized to prevent iodine deficiency. It is commonly used in everyday cooking and baking due to its uniform texture and quick dissolution. Iodized salt has a slightly metallic taste, so some cooks prefer non-iodized for delicate dishes.

# ARNIETEX SEASONING BLENDS

When developing the recipes for this book, it became apparent to me that it would be helpful to include a few seasoning blends, especially for the barbecue and grilling recipes. These blends are balanced, flavorful, delicious, and great as is; they also can serve as a foundation of flavor upon which you can lightly layer and combine your other favorite rubs to create a flavor profile that is truly yours.

When seasoning meat or coating it with a rub, there's no one exact amount of seasoning per pound or per cut. I usually season by liberal, medium, or light amounts, although I do recommend measurements in the recipes in this book in case you're not as comfortable as I am with these amounts. Practice with different quantities of blends and rubs as you cook to find your preference. To apply these blends, I prefer a shaker with holes for consistent, even coating on each part of the meat. I highly recommend making a double or triple batch of each blend and storing them in shakers or jars in a cool, dry place. They'll keep for up to 6 months.

### ARNIETEX BEEF SEASONING BLEND
2 tbsp salt
½ tsp black pepper
½ tsp granulated garlic
¼ tsp granulated onion
2 tsp chili powder

### ARNIETEX POULTRY SEASONING BLEND
2 tbsp salt
½ tsp black pepper
¼ tsp granulated garlic
¼ tsp granulated onion
½ tsp chili powder
½ tsp lemon pepper

### ARNIETEX PORK SEASONING BLEND
2 tbsp salt
2 tbsp sugar
½ tsp black pepper
¼ tsp granulated garlic
¼ tsp granulated onion
2 tsp chili powder
½ tsp smoked paprika

# SAUCES, SPRITZES, MARINADES, *AND* MORE

Flavor is often built in layers. The following sauces, marinades, and other flavor enhancers tenderize, help the cooking process, or both, all while adding complex layers of flavor to your food. Learning to use these cooking aids makes your finished dishes burst with flavor.

**ADOBOS** Adobos are flavorful marinades or sauces made from a blend of spices, vinegar, garlic, and sometimes chiles. They're commonly used in Mexican and various Latin American cuisines to soften, season, and tenderize meats and infuse deep, earthy flavors. They also can serve as a marinade base. One of the most popular and beloved adobos is the one used for al pastor dishes.

**BARBECUE SPRITZES**    Barbecue spritz is used to prevent the meat from drying out, to add a touch of flavor, and to help promote texture. This quick and easy spritz is made with ¾ cup water (bottled water preferably) and ¼ cup apple cider vinegar.

**CONSOMMÉS/BOUILLONS**    These flavor boosters come in powdered, cubed, and liquid form and are heavily used in both home and restaurant cooking. Many are loaded with tons of salt and MSG. Although I love both of those things, I like to coax natural flavors from my dishes, so I rarely use the store-bought versions. (I do like a nice homemade consommé though!)

**MARINADES**    Marinades are seasoned liquid mixtures, made with an acid, oil, herbs, or spices to tenderize and infuse flavor into meats, fish, and vegetables for anywhere from 30 minutes before cooking up to several hours and even overnight. There are a variety of marinade recipes for every cut of meat or ingredient. Acid-based marinades are made with vinegar, lemon juice, or wine and are used to tenderize and flavor. They're especially good with chicken. Enzyme-based marinades are made with pineapple or papaya, which contain natural enzymes that help break down meat fibers. They're great with tough cuts such as skirt steak. Dairy-based marinades are made with buttermilk or yogurt and are used to gently tenderize meat, often chicken or lamb.

**SAUCES**    Barbecue sauces are not common in Mexican and south Texas cooking, but they are being used more often in the past few years. In competition barbecue, a good sauce is an absolute must, and "if you're not saucin', you're not walkin'" is a common phrase in barbecue circles. Barbecue sauces are savory, sweet, tangy, and sometimes spicy condiments made from ingredients like tomatoes, vinegar, sugar, and spices to enhance the flavor of grilled or smoked meats. I used to make sauces from scratch, but today there are many perfectly great, competition-worthy barbecue sauces on the shelves and online.

**SMOKE**    The wood you smoke or grill with can be a flavor enhancer and have a big impact on the final flavor profile of your barbecue meats, veggies, and seafood, especially when smoking. Try different ones until you find the one you love. (I recommend a few in the earlier "Grills and Smokers" section.)

# CHILES 𝔸𝔑𝔇 OTHER VEGETABLES

Many chiles and other vegetables are common in Mexican kitchens and restaurants, and they're called for in many recipes in this book, too. These vegetables help define Mexican cuisine and boost the flavor—and sometimes the heat—of so many dishes.

**CHILE PEPPERS, FRESH**    Fresh chile peppers are key ingredients in Mexican cooking and add both flavor and heat to dishes. Here are a few called for in the recipes in this book:

- *Jalapeños* are perhaps the most popular and recognizable chile pepper. They're on the mild end of the heat scale, although you may occasionally find one that's particularly hot. Jalapeños have an unmistakable flavor that's great for so many recipes.

- *Serranos* are similar in appearance to jalapeños, but serranos pack a greater amount of heat. Although spicy, serranos are relatively balanced and nice for adding heat to marinades, salsas, and other dishes.

- *Habaneros* are one of the original super-hot peppers. They're small, but proceed with caution because they pack a serious amount of heat. They're usually reserved for specific applications or for super-spicy lovers, like me.

**CHILES, DRIED**    Dried chiles form the base of many traditional northern Mexican and South American dishes, adding depth, smokiness, and complexity to salsas, sauces, marinades, and more. Here are a few varieties that can provide vibrant colors and mild heat to your recipes:

- **Anchos** are dried poblano peppers with a mild to medium heat and a rich, smoky, and slightly sweet flavor. They're often used in adobos and salsas.

- **Árbol** are small, bright red chiles when fresh and turn a deeper red when dried. These chiles are *hot* and used in many recipes to add a potent kick that's full of flavor.

- **Chipotles** are smoked and dried jalapeños. They add a bold, smoky, and spicy kick to adobos, salsas, and meats.

- **Guajillos** are long, red, and mildly spicy chiles that impart a fruity, tangy flavor. They're essential in many Mexican sauces and salsas and add a wonderful smoky flavor when lightly toasted. They're similar to New Mexico and California chiles.
- **Pasillas,** known for their mild heat, have a deep, smoky flavor. They're frequently used in salsas and marinades.

**GARLIC**    There are several varieties of garlic, such as hardneck and softneck. Softneck garlic is the most common for culinary use due to its mild flavor, long shelf life, and availability. Garlic heads come in different sizes; in general, I use the standard size found in most grocery stores.

**ONIONS**    Yellow onions, known for their balanced sweetness and mild, savory flavor, are a common cooking onion. Red onions are milder and often used raw in salads or salsas. White onions have a sharper, more pungent taste, and are used in Mexican cuisine and salsas. I use medium-sized white onions the most.

**TOMATILLOS**    Tomatillos are a small, green, and tart relative of the tomato and are widely used in Mexican cooking, especially for salsas and sauces.

**TOMATOES**    In south Texas and northern Mexico, the most common tomatoes used for cooking are Roma tomatoes (or plum tomatoes). They have a meaty texture and low moisture, making them ideal for salsas, sauces, and stews. Larger, rounder vine-ripened tomatoes are nice in fresh salsas, salads, and as the base of many traditional dishes like mole and pico de gallo. I prefer Romas for just about everything for the consistent flavor they provide.

# OILS ᴀɴᴅ FATS

What oils or fats you use is a personal choice, but I encourage you experiment to find those whose flavors, smoke points (temperature at which the oil or fat begins to smoke), and health pros and cons you prefer. In general, I use avocado oil for higher-heat cooking and frying, olive oil for general cooking, and extra virgin olive oil or avocado oil for salsas. I only use peanut oil for frying turkey on Thanksgiving. And I use lard, ghee, and beef tallow as much as possible.

**PRO TIP**

*All oils can be used as cooking oils, and you can fry in any of them, too, but the best oils for frying are the ones with higher smoke points. Yes, you can fry with olive oil, but avocado, canola, and peanut oils have a higher smoke point and, therefore, will stand up to the higher temperatures and won't burn or release free radicals into your food.*

**AVOCADO OIL**    Avocado oil is a nutritious cooking oil that's high in monounsaturated and polyunsaturated fats and antioxidants with a mild flavor and neutral taste. Smoke point: ~520°F (270°C). Pros: high in monounsaturated fats; perfect for high-heat cooking. Con: typically more expensive than other oils.

**BEEF TALLOW**    Beef tallow is rich in healthy fats and resistant to oxidation, making it a great option for frying and roasting, and it has a mild beefy flavor that takes well to herbs and spices. Smoke point: 400°F (200°C) to 420°F (215°C). Pros: a natural food; has a high smoke point; adds excellent flavor. Con: high in saturated fat.

**CANOLA OIL**    Canola oil is a widely used oil with a neutral, mild flavor that helps preserve the flavor of the other ingredients. Smoke point: about 400°F (200°C). Pros: mild flavor; versatile for frying, sautéing, and baking; affordable. Cons: often processed; commonly derived from genetically modified crops.

**GHEE**    Ghee, or clarified butter, packs a slightly roasted background note, without the creamy mouthfeel of butter, but with a richer and cleaner flavor. Smoke point: 485°F (250°C). Pros: rich in nutrients and healthy fats; high smoke point; and adds great flavor. Cons: high in calories; not vegan; expensive.

**LARD**    Lard is 100 percent pork fat. It has a mild to neutral pork flavor and is great for cooking, baking, and deep-frying. Smoke point: 375°F (190°C). Pros: contains monounsaturated fats and oleic acid. Con: contains high amounts of saturated fat.

**OLIVE OIL, EXTRA VIRGIN**    Olive oil is a fruity, pungent, and strongly flavored oil (so not a neutral oil). It's great for low-heat cooking and finishing dishes. Smoke point: about 375°F (190°C). Pros: rich in antioxidants and healthy fats; adds great flavor to dressings and low-heat cooking.

# PHILOSOPHY AND PRO TIPS

★ ★ ★

To be great at anything takes a ton of practice, and this absolutely includes cooking. Here I share my most-referenced mantras and advice that I have found especially useful during my years barbecuing. If you apply the thoughts in this section consistently, you are all but guaranteed to improve, little by little, over time. Then when you look back, you will be able to see how far you've come.

## THERE AIN'T NO RIGHT WAY AND AIN'T NO WRONG WAY WHEN IT COMES TO COOKING

This has been my mantra for many years. You can approach cooking a recipe in any number of ways, and each individual cook will have their own preferences, techniques, and traditions that they will bring to the table. Old traditions and recipes are amazing, but you can add, adjust, or remove aspects of them to make them your own.

Take a look at Texas barbecue culture and its relatively recent evolution, specifically with brisket. Brisket is a huge hunk of meat that was looked down upon until the early pitmasters shared the magic of what a patient, low-and-slow, 12- to 14-hour cook would turn it into.

Traditionally, brisket was seasoned with only salt and pepper. That wasn't enough for some pitmasters. Since brisket's explosion in popularity, you now will find briskets seasoned with cumin, paprika, garlic, cayenne, coffee, chili powder, sugar, coriander, oregano, and more. And don't get me started on how cooks are serving brisket—brisket breakfast tacos, brisket burgers, brisket fideo, brisket ramen, brisket with salsa verde, and shredded brisket between buns and smothered in barbecue sauce.

There are a few ways to think about all the above. You can grind your teeth at the transgression of tradition, or you can scoot your chair up to the table and dig in. One of those ways will leave you with a big smile on your face.

I encourage you to try different things. If you take anything from this book, I hope it's the confidence to experiment with cooking, modifying, and learning to love your own favorite recipes. Make them your own, and share them with those you care about and love. I promise you that the journey is well worth it!

**MAKE IT WORK** This is another mantra of mine; it actually was the subject of the first ArnieTex video I ever posted. While speaking to a competition barbecue class, I shared one of my favorite "make it work" stories. Once at a cook-off, I was briefly distracted and the skin on my chicken completely burst and tore off the meat due to the grill's high heat. Normally this would mean a zero for the presentation score. At the time, cook-offs were my full-time job, and I wasn't about to get a zero on this bird. I sauced it, let it set, and then checked it out. It wasn't too bad! I sauced it and let it set again. Now it was actually looking pretty good! I sauced it and set it once more before plating it and turning it in. At the awards, I got first place on the chicken, which helped me win the overall cook-off and walk away as grand champion with my paycheck for the week.

I had a choice when the skin burst: call it quits or try my best. I can't express enough how important it is for y'all to embody this idea. Don't give up on the cook. You're already there. You've already committed. See it all the way through and learn the lesson. You just might surprise yourself with how great your food turns out.

**LA MANO** La mano (your hand) means "a pinch of this and a dash of that," just like your mother and grandmothers cooked. It means that as you cook more, you develop a sense and a feel for just how much seasoning to add, how much fire to have in your cooker, or how much airflow you need to get the cook done quickly or slowly. Over time, and with lots of practice, you develop a sense of smell, too, and you *know,* without even opening the lid, that the meat is ready, just by how the aroma perfumes the air. It's a skill you develop over time. It only comes by doing the work, by trying, and by making mistakes. (And we all make mistakes.) You will always be your own worst critic, and sometimes that's a good thing, but cooking both in the kitchen and outdoors should be fun. So chill out and have fun on your journey, and you'll get better with time, patience, and practice.

**GET TO KNOW YOUR BUTCHER** There are a few cuts of meat mentioned in the recipes in this book that might not be immediately available in your area. Getting to know your butcher is one way to get what you want at the meat market. I have developed good relationships with my local butchers and grocery store managers during the

Prime
Rib
8%
Chuck
26%
T-Bone
8%
Rump
3%
Short Ribs
1.5%
Sirloin
9%
Brisket
6%
Fore
Shank
4%
Plate
6.5%
Flank
4%
Round
21%
Hind
Shank
3%
CARNE
ASADA

years—I have most of their cell phone numbers on speed dial! Get to know your butchers—and be nice to them—and you will always be able to ask for special cuts. They can answer questions about cuts of meats and sometimes will let you know when the best, freshest cuts come off the truck.

**SALT TO TASTE**    As discussed earlier, there are many types and varieties of salt to pick from. Find a good-quality salt you're happy with, and use as much or as little as you like. Just because a recipe calls for 1 teaspoon or 1 tablespoon of salt doesn't mean that's what you have to add. Some people like more salt than others, and some may be on a low-sodium diet, so feel free to use more or less salt than what a recipe calls for.

**BEEF QUALITY**    We are so fortunate to have so many great meats available in a few grades. Higher grades are usually—but not always—better, so buy the best quality you can. Here are some common grades to consider:

- *Prime* is the highest grade, known for its excellent marbling, tenderness, and flavor. Prime-grade beef usually comes from younger cattle and is often served in high-end restaurants or sold at specialty butcher shops.

- *Choice-grade* beef has slightly less marbling than Prime, but it's still high quality. Choice is widely available and suitable for a variety of cooking methods. It's common in grocery stores and provides good tenderness and flavor.

- *Select-grade* beef has less marbling, making it leaner than Prime and Choice. Although still flavorful, it may not be as tender or juicy. It's often best suited for slow-cooking methods to avoid dryness.

## PRO TIP

*Wagyu and Kobe are high-end cows from Japan and, more recently, Australia that produce exceptional meat with a greater amount of marbling and a more exceptional flavor than all other beef. Many ranches in the United States raise them now, too. Wagyu and Kobe are expensive, but I think everyone should try them at least once if their budget allows.*

**FLIPPITY FLIP**    I started saying this years ago when competing with fajitas and steaks. At first, it was just a personal observation but then science confirmed what I saw. When grilling, heat pushes moisture up to the top of the meat, where it evaporates fairly quickly—*unless* you flip, flip, flippity flip. Flip early and often, as soon as the moisture begins to pool on top. You'll still get that beautiful delicious maillard-reaction char, but you'll also be rewarded with a much juicier cut of meat.

**REST MEAT**    Resting meat after cooking it helps the meat retain its juices and enhance its moisture. If meat is cut into immediately after being removed from the heat, the juices escape, resulting in a drier texture. Resting allows the juices to reabsorb throughout the meat's fibers, keeping it moist and flavorful. Resting times vary based on the meat type and thickness, but for optimal results, rest small cuts for 5 to 10 minutes, larger roasts for up to 20 to 30 minutes, and smoked briskets for preferably 3 or 4 hours.

**USE A THERMOMETER**    I can't stress enough the importance of consistent perfection when it comes to cooking meats. You will get it right every time if you use a meat thermometer. If chefs and cooks who make their living in the kitchen or by the big smokers cooking hundreds of briskets a week use thermometers, you should, too. It's not about having experience cooking, it's about being perfect every time.

**FIRE CONTROL**    When cooking on the grill, it's all about fuel, combustion, and airflow. Using too much fuel and lots of air will result in a raging-hot fire. Not enough of either, and you may never finish cooking without a reload. Learn to add the right amount of fuel, and set the airflow and exhaust to maintain steady, consistent temperature. It takes practice, and you'll get better with each cook, so just get outside and do it.

**WEATHER AND ELEVATION**    Both the weather and the elevation at which you're cooking can affect your cook times, when you're cooking indoors and out. Humid air starves a fire of oxygen, and higher elevations have less oxygen, so when cooking in those conditions, be sure to open the air vents wide.

**COOKING TEMPERATURES**    Every stove, grill, and cooker is different—275°F (140°C) on one grill is not the same as 275°F (140°C) on another—so know yours and how it cooks. Many grills don't have the gauge at the level of the meat, so even if the gauge reads 275°F (140°C), the temperature at the meat level might be 250°F (120°C) or 245°F (118°C). Checking both the gauge and the temperature of the grate, using an infrared thermometer will ensure the best results. An oven thermometer placed inside your pit or grill is also a great option to check and monitor cooking temperatures.

# 2
# SALSAS, SAUCES, *AND* MARINADES

# PICO DE GALLO

**PREP TIME**
10 to 15 minutes
plus 30 minutes for
flavors to blend

**COOK TIME**
none

**MAKES**
about 4 cups

Pico de gallo (or literally "rooster's beak" in Spanish) is one of the most requested salsas in Tex-Mex and Mexican restaurants, and for good reason: This cool, refreshing dish tastes amazing and is rich in vitamins and nutrients. The key to making great pico is patience. After you've combined all the ingredients, let the dish sit in the refrigerator for at least 30 minutes or up to 2 hours to allow the flavors to blend.

9 Roma tomatoes, diced

2 tsp salt

½ medium white onion, diced

3 serrano chiles or 2 jalapeños, stem removed and diced

1 bunch of cilantro, stems removed, roughly chopped

Juice of 1 lime, or juice of 1 lemon for a different flavor twist

1 garlic clove, minced (optional)

1 medium avocado, peeled, pitted, and diced (optional)

1 Add the tomatoes to a large bowl that can hold all the ingredients. If you have juice from the tomatoes, add that to the bowl, too.

2 Add the salt, and stir to dissolve.

3 Add the onion, chiles, cilantro, lime juice, garlic (if using), and avocado (if using). Mix well.

4 Place in the refrigerator, and let sit for at least 30 minutes or up to 2 hours.

5 Serve with Totopos (page 211) on the side for scooping.

## COOKING NOTES

*Take your pico de gallo up a notch by adding some cubed avocado. Avocado makes the tomato and lime juices creamier and brings a whole different kind of deliciousness to the dish. For more heat, you can add additional serranos or swap them for habaneros.*

*Pico de gallo is best eaten fresh, the same day it is prepared. If you do have leftovers, store in an airtight container in the refrigerator and eat within a day.*

SALSA ROJA—BOILED

SALSA ROJA—RANCHERA

SALSA ROJA—TAQUERIA

PREP TIME
5 minutes

COOK TIME
10 minutes

MAKES
about 2 cups

# SALSA ROJA–RANCHERA

This is my favorite breakfast salsa, but it can be served anytime of day with tacos, plates, or chips. It's simple but fantastic. Try this warm salsa ranchera alongside a breakfast plate or over your eggs, and you'll see what I mean.

★ ★ ★

2 tbsp canola oil

¼ medium white onion, diced

2 garlic cloves, minced

1 serrano chile, stem removed and chopped

4 Roma tomatoes, diced

½ tsp salt

1 Heat a 10-inch (25.5cm) skillet over medium heat, and add the oil. When the oil is hot, add the onion and sauté until translucent, about 2 minutes.

2 Add the garlic, and sauté for 1 more minute.

3 Add the serrano and tomatoes, and sauté until the tomatoes are cooked through and soft, about 5 minutes.

4 Add the salt, and stir to incorporate.

5 There are two methods to bring it all together: You can either use a potato masher to mash all the ingredients together in the skillet to a semi-chunky consistency and texture, thinning the salsa with a splash of water for a looser consistency if you like, or you can remove the skillet from heat and cool for 5 minutes before adding the ingredients to a blender, along with ½ cup of water, and blending to a fine, loose consistency.

6 Serve hot from the blender. Store any leftovers in an airtight container in the refrigerator for up to 5 days.

## COOKING NOTES

*For a milder heat level, you can substitute a jalapeño for the serrano chile.*

PREP TIME
5 minutes

COOK TIME
10 minutes

MAKES
about 3 cups

# SALSA ROJA—BOILED

This is my go-to, quick-and-delicious salsa roja that's perfect served with chips or atop any dish. Every salsa varies a bit, depending on the restaurant or cook. Many salsa rojas contain onion; however, this recipe does not, in order to focus on the tomato-forward umami flavor of the dish. If you prefer onion in your salsa roja, you can add ¼ of a medium white onion.

★ ★ ★

5 Roma tomatoes

2 serrano chiles

2 garlic cloves

10 sprigs of cilantro, leaves only

½ tsp salt, or to taste

1  Add the tomatoes and serranos to a stockpot, fill with just enough water to cover the vegetables, and set over medium-high heat. Bring to a boil and then reduce the heat to medium-low and simmer until the tomatoes start to peel and are soft, about 10 minutes. The serranos should be opaque by this time, too. Turn off the heat.

2  Add the garlic to the stockpot to soften it for efficient blending.

3  Let the ingredients cool in the stockpot for 5 minutes.

4  To a blender, add 2 of the tomatoes, the garlic, and the salt. Blend on high until a fine puree forms to ensure the garlic is evenly distributed. Add the remaining 3 tomatoes, serranos, and cilantro, and pulse or blend to your desired consistency.

5  Taste the salsa, adjust the salt if needed, and serve. Store any leftovers in an airtight container in the refrigerator for up to 5 days.

## COOKING NOTES

*For a milder heat level, substitute 2 jalapeños for the serrano chiles.*

PREP TIME
5 minutes

COOK TIME
10 minutes

MAKES
2–2½ cups

# SALSA ROJA–TAQUERIA

It's red, and it's hot! This creamy salsa roja turns a bright orange after emulsification and is the other half to the salsa verde often served in taquerias. It is absolutely superb on street-style tacos and equally delicious with breakfast tacos or classic plates like carne guisada.

★ ★ ★

3 Roma tomatoes

7 red jalapeños

10 chiles de árbol

3 garlic cloves

3 tbsp olive or vegetable oil, for blending

1 tsp salt, or to taste

1  Add the tomatoes, jalapeños, and the chiles de árbol to a stockpot, fill with just enough water to cover the vegetables, and set over medium-high heat. Bring to a boil.

2  Reduce the heat to medium-low and simmer until the tomatoes start to peel, about 10 minutes. Turn off the heat.

3  Add the garlic to the stockpot, and let it soften for 5 minutes.

4  Transfer the vegetables to a blender, add the salt, and blend until smooth.

5  With the blender on medium, slowly drizzle in the oil until the salsa is fully emulsified.

6  Taste the salsa, adjust the salt if needed, and serve. Store any leftovers in an airtight container in the refrigerator for up to 3 days.

# SALSA VERDE—BASE

**PREP TIME**
5 minutes

**COOK TIME**
15 minutes

**MAKES**
about 2½ cups

This is my absolute favorite salsa. It's super easy to make, and if you can tolerate the heat, it's extremely delicious. It's also a great base for other salsas; adds a wonderful flavor to tacos, caldos, asados, guisos, menudos, and ceviches without changing the flavor profile of the dishes; and is a nice addition to any dish with masa, like tamales or gorditas. I've been known to even spice up my salads with it. Note that this salsa verde is not the more popular version made with tomatillos and onion. This is a prominent regional dish found in Northern Mexico and South Texas and is served at restaurants that know their patrons would like something with a kick.

10 serrano chiles
10 jalapeños

3 garlic cloves

1 tsp salt

1 Add the serranos and jalapeños to a stockpot, and fill with enough water to cover the chiles by 1 to 2 inches (2.5–5cm). Set over medium heat, and bring to a boil. Reduce the heat to low, and boil for 10 minutes.

2 After the 10-minute boil, shut off the heat, throw in the garlic to soften for 5 minutes, then proceed to step 3.

3 Strain out the chiles and garlic, and reserve some of the cooking water. Allow the chiles and garlic to cool for 5 minutes.

4 Add the chiles, garlic, salt, and about ½ cup of the cooking water to a blender. Pulse the blender a few times to encourage an even chop and then pulse intermittently until your desired consistency. If the salsa verde is too thick, add more cooking water. For a smoother texture, blend longer.

5 Serve on any dish, in tacos, or with a bowl of chips. Store any leftovers in an airtight container in the refrigerator for up to 2 weeks.

## COOKING NOTES

*For a creamy texture, slowly add ¼ cup olive or vegetable oil to the blender in step 4 and blend on high until fully emulsified. Also, be aware that jalapeños and serranos can be a bit unpredictable when it comes to heat level, which can depend on the maturation time on the vine. Serranos in general are considerably hotter than jalapeños, so adjust this recipe accordingly for your preferences.*

SALSA VERDE–TOMATILLOS

SALSA VERDE–BASE

SALSA VERDE–TAQUERIA

PREP TIME
5 minutes

COOK TIME
10 minutes

MAKES
about 3½ cups

# SALSA VERDE—TOMATILLOS

This iconic, tomatillo-based version of salsa verde is a must-have in every kitchen. The tomatillos bring a bright, sharp, and somewhat tangy flavor, and when cooked and blended, they create a loose-textured salsa that's perfect for smothering chilaquiles, pairing with pork, or topping tacos. The ingredients called for here create a salsa that packs a lot of flavor—and a lot of heat. For a milder version, omit either the serrano chiles or chiles de árbol.

★ ★ ★

7 tomatillos, husks removed

2 serrano chiles

2 jalapeños

5 chiles de árbol

3 garlic cloves

1 bunch of cilantro

1 tsp salt

1  Bring a large pot of water to a mild boil over medium-high heat. Add the tomatillos, serranos, jalapeños, chiles de árbol, and garlic to the boiling water, and cook until the tomatillos develop a soft texture and are slightly opaque all around, about 10 minutes. Turn off the heat.

2  Transfer the tomatillos, chiles, and garlic to a blender. Allow the vegetables to cool for 5 minutes.

3  Add the cilantro and salt to the blender, and blend until your desired consistency. If you prefer a looser salsa, add ¼ to ½ cup of the cooking water to the blender and blend again.

4  Serve. Store any leftovers in an airtight container in the refrigerator for up to 5 days.

## COOKING NOTES

*The tomatillos, chiles, and garlic in this salsa verde can be roasted instead of boiled. See the following Salsa Verde—Taqueria recipe (page 43) for roasting instructions.*

*If you prefer less heat, you can omit the chiles de árbol and/or serrano chiles.*

PREP TIME
5 minutes

COOK TIME
20 minutes

MAKES
about 2 cups

# SALSA VERDE—TAQUERIA

This version of salsa verde is another simple yet fundamental recipe and technique to add to your arsenal of heat. The white onion adds a note of sweetness that completely changes the flavor while still holding true to a traditional recipe. The emulsified texture of this salsa verde is commonly found in taquerias or served with street tacos. This recipe takes inspiration from that tradition.

12 jalapeños
½ medium white onion, quartered

4 tbsp olive or vegetable oil
8 garlic cloves

1 tsp salt

1  Preheat the oven to 400°F (200°C).

2  Place the jalapeños and onion on a baking sheet, and drizzle with 1 tablespoon of oil. Toss to ensure the vegetables are evenly coated in the oil.

3  Roast in the oven for 10 minutes. Remove from the oven, and flip over the vegetables.

4  Add the garlic to the baking sheet, return it to the oven, and roast for 10 more minutes. Remove the vegetables from the oven and set aside to rest for 5 minutes.

5  Transfer the roasted vegetables to a blender, add the salt and ½ cup of water. Blend for 20 seconds, and check for consistency. Add more water if necessary. You want a slightly loose but not watery consistency.

6  With the blender on medium, slowly add the remaining 3 tablespoons of oil to emulsify the salsa. Increase the speed to high for 30 seconds or until the salsa is smoothly blended and fully emulsified.

7  Transfer to a bowl or a squirt bottle, and serve. Store any leftovers in an airtight container in the refrigerator for up to 5 days

## COOKING NOTES

*Although popular for street tacos, this salsa verde is also great with any type of taco or traditional meal. Roasting the vegetables adds a distinct flavor to this salsa verde, but you can boil the ingredients instead for similar results. See the earlier Salsa Verde—Tomatillos recipe (page 42) for boiling instructions.*

PREP TIME
5 minutes

COOK TIME
20 minutes

MAKES
about 3½ cups

# SALSA VERDE—AGUACATE

This salsa verde is simple to prepare but far from basic. By adding a little bit of "green gold"—aka avocado—to a base of tomatillos, you are rewarded with a wonderful, creamy-finish salsa verde that provides a nice contrast to the crunch of totopos and is great layered on top of your favorite tacos.

★ ★ ★

5 tomatillos, husks removed
2 jalapeños
2 garlic cloves
¼ medium white onion

¼ cup plus 1 tbsp olive or vegetable oil
15 sprigs of cilantro, stems removed (optional)

1 tsp salt, or to taste
1 ripe avocado, peeled and pitted

1  Preheat the oven to 400°F (200°C).

2  Place the tomatillos, jalapeños, garlic, and onion on a baking sheet, and drizzle with 1 tablespoon of oil. Toss to ensure the vegetables are evenly coated in the oil.

3  Roast in the oven for 10 minutes. Remove from the oven, flip over the vegetables, and roast for 10 more minutes. Remove from the oven, and allow the vegetables to cool for 5 minutes.

4  Add the roasted tomatillos, jalapeños, garlic, and onion to a blender along with the cilantro (if using) and salt. Pulse 3 or 4 times to begin incorporating the ingredients.

5  Add the avocado, and blend on high. While blending, add the remaining ¼ cup of oil to begin emulsifying the salsa. Blend on high for 1 minute to fully incorporate and emulsify.

6  Pour into a bowl and serve. Store any leftovers in an airtight container in the refrigerator for up to 3 days.

## PRO TIPS

*If the salsa is too thick to blend thoroughly, add water, 1 tablespoon at a time, and blend again. Repeat this process until you achieve the desired consistency.*

# SALSA TAQUERA

**PREP TIME**
7 minutes

**COOK TIME**
12 minutes

**MAKES**
about 3½ cups

Salsa taquera literally translates as "salsa for tacos," and hundreds, if not thousands, of salsas bear this name. This is one of the most generalized salsas that embodies the "ain't no right way, ain't no wrong way" spirit of cooking. But a salsa taquera must be versatile enough for any kind of taco, not just for pairing with certain dishes. Therefore, every taquero will have their own salsa recipe they believe is best served with their food. This is mine. It's a salsa I serve for breakfast, lunch, and dinner.

★ ★ ★

1 tbsp vegetable oil
10 chiles de árbol
¼ medium white onion, sliced

5 Roma tomatoes
3 serrano chiles
3 garlic cloves

1 tsp salt
¼ tsp black pepper

1   Heat a 10-inch (25.5cm) skillet over medium heat, and add the oil. When the oil is hot, add the chiles de árbol and fry, stirring often, for 30 to 40 seconds. Be careful not to overcook them, which will result in a bitter flavor. Transfer the chiles to a blender.

2   Add the onion, tomatoes, serranos, and garlic to the skillet, and cook, stirring and flipping them to develop color and char evenly throughout, about 5 minutes.

3   Remove the garlic, and transfer it to the blender with the chiles de árbol.

4   Continue cooking and stirring the remaining ingredients in the skillet for 5 more minutes and then transfer to the blender. Add the salt and pepper, and allow the ingredients to cool for 5 minutes before blending.

5   Pulse the ingredients a few times and then blend on medium to develop a smooth consistency. Adjust with ¼ cup water if you prefer your salsa a bit looser.

6   Serve with your favorite tacos. Store any leftovers in an airtight container in the refrigerator for up to 5 days.

# CREAMY HABANERO SALSA

**PREP TIME**
3 minutes

**COOK TIME**
5 minutes

**MAKES**
about 1¼ cups

This one is for the salsa warriors. Habaneros are the original superhot chiles, before it was a thing to engineer chiles to unenjoyable levels of heat. (See Pro Tips.) With that said, habaneros are also very special. When incorporated well, they bring a sweet and citrusy note to the salsa that is enjoyable and very spicy. This salsa is blended and emulsified thoroughly into a delicious, creamy finish that's best served in moderation.

1 tbsp plus ¼ cup vegetable oil

25 orange habanero chiles

3 garlic cloves

1 tsp salt

3 tbsp white or apple cider vinegar

1 Heat a 10-inch (25.5cm) skillet over medium-high heat, and add 1 tablespoon of the oil. When the oil is hot, add the habaneros and garlic, and sauté for 5 to 6 minutes.

2 Transfer the habaneros and garlic to the blender. Add the salt, vinegar, and ¼ cup water, and blend into a smooth puree. With the blender on medium, drizzle in the remaining ¼ cup of the vegetable oil until the salsa is fully emulsified. If the salsa is too thick for your liking, add water, a tablespoon at a time, until the salsa reaches the desired consistency.

3 Serve in moderation. Store any leftovers in an airtight container in the refrigerator for up to 5 days

## PRO TIPS

*Habanero chiles pack so much heat, be very careful when making this salsa. Use gloves when handling them, be careful not to touch your face or eyes, and wash your hands thoroughly after touching the habaneros.*

*It's also a good idea to ensure your range hood is running to extract the air over your stove, otherwise you might wind up coughing and crying!*

# FIRE-ROASTED SALSA

**PREP TIME**
5 minutes

**COOK TIME**
10 minutes over a
medium-hot fire

**MAKES**
4–5 cups

A fire-roasted salsa is simply one of the best accompaniments to any carne asada. After all, the fire is already lit, so you might as well take advantage of it and whip up this situationally delicious recipe to serve along with your spread of sides. Cooking this salsa over the fire adds a smoky note of flavor that pairs perfectly with the grilled meats.

5 tomatillos, husks removed

3 jalapeños (or serranos for more heat)

3 Roma tomatoes

½ medium white onion

3 garlic cloves

15 chiles de árbol

1 tsp salt

1 Place the tomatillos, jalapeños, tomatoes, and onion over a medium-hot fire. Cook, rotating the vegetables every 2 minutes as char develops evenly around them, about 10 minutes. Remove the vegetables from the heat when they are soft and lightly but evenly charred.

2 For the garlic: Place the garlic cloves on the grill at the same time as the tomatillos, jalapeños, tomatoes, and onion in step 1, but rotate it more frequently as the char develops. Remove after 5 minutes or as soon as they are charred on all sides.

3 Place the chiles de árbol in a spider strainer to prevent these thin, small chiles from falling through the grill grate and into the coals. Set the spider directly onto the coals, and shake it in a circular motion to cook the chiles. These only need about 15 to 30 seconds over the coals with frequent shaking. Any longer runs the risk of them burning and getting a bitter flavor.

4 Place all the ingredients in a blender along with the salt, and pulse to your desired consistency.

5 Serve. Store any leftovers in an airtight container in the refrigerator for up to 5 days.

## COOKING NOTES

*This recipe is great with the juice of a lightly roasted lemon or lime blended with the other ingredients. Cutting the citrus in half and roasting it with the vegetables helps loosen the juice in the citrus and brings a unique, tangy flavor to the salsa that pairs superbly with grilled proteins. For an even more exceptional finish, you can add 1 large avocado, peeled, pitted, and cubed, to the blended salsa just before serving. The avocado will bring a creamier texture to the finished salsa.*

PREP TIME
7 minutes

COOK TIME
none

MAKES
about 5 cups

# SALSA CHIPOTLE EN ADOBO

It's amazing how a single ingredient can transform the entire flavor and eating experience of a salsa. When I had my restaurant, our house salsa contained a secret ingredient: chipotles in adobo sauce. Adding this ingredient in a conventional salsa roja consistently earned pleasantly surprised reactions from diners. This salsa is guaranteed to stand out and be the hit of any party or carne asada where it's served. The inclusion of diced canned tomatoes is a common restaurant move that both stretches out the salsa and adds another surprising ingredient to make a truly unique bite. I know I said this in another salsa recipe, but this is also one of my favorite salsas to eat with a big ol' bag of chips!

5 Roma tomatoes, diced
½ medium white onion, diced
3 serrano chiles, diced

1 × 12 oz (340g) can diced tomatoes, with juice
2 chipotles in adobo sauce

1 tsp salt
2 garlic cloves, diced
1 bunch of cilantro

1 Add half of the Roma tomatoes, half of the onion, half of the serranos, half of the canned tomatoes with juice, both chipotles, and the salt to a blender.

2 Blend on high until a fine puree, about 1 minute. This creates a great liquid base.

3 Add the remaining ingredients to the blender, along with the garlic and cilantro, and pulse the salsa to a medium, chunky texture or to your preference.

4 Serve. This salsa is best enjoyed during the first day. Store any leftovers in an airtight container in the refrigerator for up to 2 days.

PREP TIME
5 minutes

COOK TIME
10 minutes

MAKES
about 3 cups

# SALSA CHILE PIQUÍN

I know I say this a lot, but seriously, this is one of my favorite salsas. The chile piquín has a nutty flavor that packs big heat and versatility, and it's not uncommon for me to alternate bites of food with one (or two) chile piquín. When dried, these chiles can be crushed and shaken over dishes for a major boost of flavor and heat. These are also known as chile del monte and can be substituted with the more accessible chile tepín. This recipe is a hot one and focuses on the chiles' flavor and heat paired with the balance of the Roma tomatoes. This salsa goes great with a bowl of chips, on tacos, or mixed into individual servings of guisos for a pop of flavor and punch of heat.

★ ★ ★

5 Roma tomatoes
¼ medium white onion

3 garlic cloves
10 chiles piquín

1½ tsp salt, or to taste

1   Add the tomatoes, onion, and garlic to a 4-quart (3.8-liter) saucepan, fill with just enough water to cover the vegetables, and set over medium-heat. Bring to a boil, and cook until the tomatoes begin to peel and are soft, about 10 minutes.

2   Turn off the heat, add the chiles piquín, and allow the vegetables to cool in the pot for 5 minutes.

3   Transfer all the vegetables to a blender, and add the salt. Blend or pulse to your desired consistency.

4   Taste the salsa, adjust the salt if needed, and serve. Store any leftovers in an airtight container in the refrigerator for up to 5 days.

# SALSA PUYA

**PREP TIME**
7 minutes

**COOK TIME**
15 minutes

**MAKES**
about 3 cups

The chile puya packs a bright, fruity, smoky flavor, but it is sometimes overshadowed by its peer, the chile guajillo. I love the puya because it brings more heat and a brighter flavor to a salsa than the guajillo and it's another one of those dried chiles that, due its lesser-known reputation, is often pleasantly surprising to the uninitiated. When toasted, it offers a distinct, pleasant, smoky, and fruity aroma that builds as you prepare the salsa. This recipe combines puya and guajillo to introduce you to the flavor and creates a base upon which you can add more puyas if you like. The chiles de árbol pack plenty of heat; if you prefer a milder salsa, reduce the chiles de árbol by half or more.

2 tbsp cooking oil

20 chiles de árbol

3 chiles guajillo, deseeded

5 chiles puya

10 tomatillos, husks removed

3 garlic cloves

1 tsp salt

1 Heat a 12-inch (30.5cm) skillet over medium-high heat, and add the oil. When the oil is hot, add the chiles de árbol, guajillo, and puya, and cook, stirring often, until soft and evenly toasted, 1 or 2 minutes max. You want to toast the chiles quickly but be sure not to overcook them. Transfer the chiles to a blender.

2 Add the tomatillos and garlic to the skillet, and fry. Rotate, flip, and turn the vegetables often to ensure they cook evenly all the way through until soft, 5 to 10 minutes. The garlic will be fully cooked in 4 or 5 minutes. Remove garlic when soft and transfer to the blender along with the salt. Remove the tomatillos when they're soft and beginning to peel, transfer to the blender, and allow to cool for 5 minutes.

3 Add ¼ cup water to the blender and blend on high for 1 minute or until the salsa is finely pureed. If large chile flakes are still present, blend for 2 minutes more or until the flakes are fully incorporated. If the salsa is still too thick for your liking, add additional water in small amounts until the desired consistency is reached.

4 Serve on tacos, breakfast eggs, in soups or stews, or with your favorite chips. Store any leftovers in an airtight container in the refrigerator for up to 5 days.

# SALSA MACHA

**PREP TIME**
20 minutes

**COOK TIME**
20 minutes

**MAKES**
about 2 cups

This is an oil-based salsa that is made with several interesting ingredients. It's nutty and garlicky and contains a blend of chiles that yields a smooth yet crunchy texture perfect for drizzling over tacos or ceviche tostadas and into caldos. You can adjust the heat level as you prepare the salsa to make it perfect for your preference. This version is between hot and mild.

- 2 cups avocado oil (or your preferred oil), divided
- ¼ cup unsalted peanuts
- 1 tbsp sesame seeds
- 3–4 garlic cloves
- 10 chiles guajillo, deseeded
- 2 chiles ancho, deseeded
- 5 chiles de árbol
- ½ tsp salt
- ¼ tsp dried Mexican oregano
- 3 tbsp white or apple cider vinegar

1  Heat a 10-inch (25.5cm) skillet over medium heat, and add ½ cup of the oil. When the oil is hot, add the peanuts, sesame seeds, and garlic, and cook until slightly roasted on all sides, about 1 minute. Transfer all ingredients, including the oil, to a bowl to cool.

2  Add another ½ cup of the oil to the skillet. When the oil is hot, add the chiles guajillo, and cook, flipping frequently, until lightly toasted and softened, about 2 minutes. Transfer the chiles guajillo and oil to a bowl. Next, add the chiles ancho to the skillet and repeat the cooking process. Finally, repeat the process to cook the chiles de árbol. Allow all the chiles to cool for 5 minutes.

3  To a blender, add ½ cup of the oil and the salt, oregano, and vinegar. Transfer the toasted nuts, seeds, and chiles to a blender. Pulse the blender 3 to 5 times in order to start breaking down the ingredients, then blend on low for 20 to 30 seconds and check for consistency. If you prefer your salsa thinner, add the remaining ½ cup of oil, 1 tablespoon at a time, and blend on low for another 30 seconds.

4  Serve immediately. Store any leftovers in an airtight container at room temperature for up to 2 weeks. For a longer shelf life, store in the refrigerator for up to 1 month.

## COOKING NOTES

*As the salsa stands, the ingredients will settle on the bottom of the container. Simply give the salsa a stir before serving to help reincorporate.*

*If you like, you can increase the amount of peanuts to ⅓ cup and reserve some after frying. Roughly chop the peanuts and add to the salsa after blending to a smooth puree in step 3 and pulse a few times. This will create some chunky, crunchy bites in the middle of the smooth salsa.*

PREP TIME
10 minutes

COOK TIME
15 minutes

MAKES
about 4 cups

# CHILE GUAJILLO SAUCE

This sauce is the base of my mother's asados, menudos, and enchiladas; it's also great for chile colorado. Because the sauce is primarily made from chiles guajillo, it has a slightly smoky and sweet flavor, making it perfect for building upon in any direction you choose.

15 chiles guajillo, deseeded

2 chiles ancho, deseeded

½ medium white onion, quartered

6 garlic cloves

5 chiles de árbol

2 tsp salt

1 Rinse the chiles guajillo and ancho well in cool water, and place them in a stockpot.

2 Add the onion, garlic, and chiles de árbol to the pot; fill with just enough water to cover the vegetables; and set over medium-high heat. Bring to a slow boil, and cook for 10 minutes.

3 Turn off the heat and allow the ingredients to sit for 5 minutes to completely soften.

4 Transfer the cooked vegetables to a blender. Reserve 2 cups of the cooking water.

5 Add the cooking water and salt to the blender, and blend on high for 1 minute or until smooth. You want the sauce to have a thick consistency that is just slightly loose.

6 Using a sieve, pour the liquid out of the blender and strain out any chili flakes and pulp. Use the back of a spoon to press the liquid from the chunks until you have expressed all the liquid. You should be left with a completely smooth sauce.

7 Use in your preferred recipe from this book. Store any leftovers in an airtight container in the refrigerator for up to 5 days.

## COOKING NOTES

*Be sure to use fresh chiles that are not too dry and crusty. The older the chiles are, the less flavor they have. Also, some cooks using modern high-speed blenders prefer not to strain the sauce in step 6. This is entirely up to you.*

# AL PASTOR ADOBO

**PREP TIME**
10 minutes

**COOK TIME**
10 minutes

**MAKES**
about 6 cups
(enough for
12 to 15 lb/5.5 to
7kg of pork)

This recipe is bright and bursting with the deep, complex flavor that gives tacos al pastor their legendary reputation. Don't be too worried about the long list of ingredients; each has its place and contributes to the overall marinade. Although this is most commonly used for tacos al pastor, you can use this to baste grilled pork steaks or smoked pork ribs or as a marinade for chicken fajitas.

15 chiles guajillo, deseeded

4 chiles ancho, deseeded

3 to 5 chiles de árbol, or to taste, deseeded (deseeding optional)

½ medium white onion, quartered

6 garlic cloves

1 bay leaf

½ tsp dried Mexican oregano

4 whole cloves

1 small cinnamon stick

½ cup chopped pineapple

1 cup fresh or canned pineapple juice

2 tbsp or 2 oz (55g) achiote paste

2 canned chipotles in adobo sauce

3 tbsp apple cider vinegar

2 tbsp salt

1  Bring a medium saucepan of water to a slow boil over medium-high heat.

2  Add the chiles guajillo, chiles ancho, chiles de árbol, onion, garlic, and bay leaf to the saucepan, and cook, stirring, for 5 minutes.

3  Turn off the heat and allow the vegetables to sit for 5 minutes to continue to soften.

4  Remove the bay leaf, and reserve 2 cups of the cooking water.

5  Transfer the cooked vegetables to a blender along with 1 cup of the cooking water. Add the oregano, cloves, cinnamon stick, pineapple, pineapple juice, achiote, chipotles, vinegar, and salt to the blender, and blend on high until smooth, mostly thick, and slightly runny. If you need to thin it out, add a bit more of the reserved cooking water and blend again for 15 seconds.

6  Use in your preferred recipe. Store any leftovers in an airtight container in the refrigerator for up to 3 days.

## COOKING NOTES

*When using this adobo to marinade meat, I recommend not seasoning your meats after because this marinade packs plenty of flavor and salt. If needed, you can shake a light coating of your favorite rub onto your cooked meat for an added pop of flavor. Also, most modern high-powered blenders do a great job making purees. Some older blenders may need to run a bit longer to fully incorporate the ingredients. The goal is to have no large flakes of chile, cloves, or cinnamon stick in the adobo. If you are using an older blender, you can soak the chiles a bit longer to ensure they're thoroughly softened before blending.*

# RED CARNICERÍA MARINADE

**PREP TIME**
20 minutes

**COOK TIME**
none

**SERVES**
enough for 4 to 5
pounds (2–2.25kg)
of meat

This is my version of the famous red carnicería (meat market) marinade. Many Mexican and Latino grocery stores and meat markets are known for their counters being stacked from end to end with a variety of beef ribs, fajitas, chicken, and pork cuts, all slathered in this red marinade, ready to grill. The bright red color comes from the use of achiote (annatto), which can be found at your local carnicería, in most grocery stores in the Mexican/Latino isles, and online. I recommend using the blocks of paste, and not the liquid, because it often contains other ingredients not needed for this recipe.

¼ cup fresh orange juice

¼ cup fresh pineapple juice

½ cup lime juice

1 tbsp apple cider vinegar

¼ cup olive oil

1 tbsp salt

1 tbsp black pepper

1 tsp granulated garlic

1 tsp granulated onion

1 tsp dried Mexican oregano

½ tsp ground cumin

2 tbsp smoked paprika

2 tsp chili powder

3 tbsp achiote paste

1   Whisk together the orange juice, pineapple juice, lime juice, and vinegar in a small bowl for 1 minute. Add the olive oil, and whisk again for 1 minute. Pour the mixture into a blender.

2   Add the salt, pepper, granulated garlic, granulated onion, oregano, cumin, paprika, chili powder, and achiote to the blender, and blend until all the ingredients are evenly incorporated, about 1 minute.

3   Place your choice of meat in a large, food-safe container. Pour the marinade over the meat and slather to ensure that it covers the meat evenly on all sides. Marinate in the refrigerator overnight or for at least 6 to 8 hours before cooking.

PREP TIME
15 minutes

COOK TIME
none

SERVES
enough for 3 to
5 pounds (1.35 to
2.25kg) of meat

# GREEN FAJITA MARINADE

There are three main marinades in Tex-Mex cooking. Acidic and enzymatic marinades focus on breaking down proteins for tenderizing by using ingredients like vinegar and citrus or fruit juices. Oil-based marinades combine herbs and spices with a base of oil that covers the meat. This recipe is a combination of all three, plus a little extra so you can wow your family and friends.

3 tomatillos, husks removed and quartered

2 jalapeños, quartered

½ medium white onion, quartered

2 garlic cloves, smashed

1 lemon

1 lime

½ cup orange juice

½ cup pineapple juice

½ cup fresh cilantro

¼ cup fresh parsley

1 tbsp vinegar

2 tsp salt

½ tsp black pepper

1 tsp ground cumin

1 tsp dried Mexican oregano

½ cup olive oil

1  Add the tomatillos, jalapeños, onion, and garlic to a blender.

2  Cut the lemon and lime in half, remove the seeds, and juice both into the blender. Set aside the lemon peels (both halves).

3  Add the orange juice, pineapple juice, cilantro, parsley, vinegar, salt, pepper, cumin, oregano, and oil to the blender, and blend for 30 seconds. Pour the marinade into a large food-safe container.

4  Roughly chop the reserved lemon peels, and add it to the marinade.

5  Add your choice of meat to the marinade, and submerge to fully cover the meat. Marinate in the refrigerator for at least 2 to 4 hours before cooking or up to 8 to 12 hours for best results.

# CHILE TOREADOS

**PREP TIME**
1 minute

**COOK TIME**
2 or 3 minutes

**SERVES**
1 or 2

These fried and blistered chiles are a popular way to amp up the heat, and diners in Mexican restaurants often request a chile toreado with their meal, especially if the house salsa doesn't pack enough heat. Jalapeños are most commonly used, but for those who are brave enough, serranos also work well.

1 tbsp olive or vegetable oil        2 jalapeños or serrano chiles

1   Heat a 10-inch (25.5cm) skillet or griddle over medium-high heat, and add the oil. When the oil is hot, carefully add the jalapeños to the skillet to sauté.

2   Toss and flip the jalapeños frequently, in about 30-second intervals, to ensure even cooking on all sides. When the jalapeños have developed a slight blister on all sides, they're ready to be served.

3   Remove the jalapeños from the skillet, allow to cool for 1 minute, and serve.

## COOKING NOTES

*If you prefer, you can fry the jalapeños in oil instead of pan-frying, a technique common in restaurants. Drop the jalapeños in hot frying oil for a few seconds until their skin starts to blister. Carefully remove the jalapeños from the oil and transfer to a heat-safe surface to cool for 1 minute before serving.*

# SALSA TATEMADA

**PREP TIME**
5 minutes

**COOK TIME**
10 minutes

**MAKES**
about 3 cups

Tatemada translates roughly as "roasted," "toasted," "charred," or "blistered." This can be accomplished over high heat from a charcoal grill, over a gas stove flame, on a griddle, or my preferred method, which is in a 10- or 12-inch (25.5cm or 30.5cm) skillet over direct heat. The beauty of salsa tatemada is that the ingredients can be as basic or as complex as you like, as long as they're charred. The charring adds a smoky flavor to the ingredients, transforming the flavor of the salsa and providing a unique tasting experience with totopos, fajitas, grilled meats, or seafood. This is also frequently served for breakfast alongside barbacoa and carnitas.

5 Roma tomatoes

2 jalapeños

¼ medium white onion

2 garlic cloves

1 chile guajillo, deseeded

5 chiles de árbol

½ tsp salt

Juice of ½ lime

1  Heat a 10-inch (25.5cm) skillet over medium heat. When the skillet is hot, add the tomatoes and jalapeños, and cook until evenly charred, about 5 minutes. Transfer the vegetables to a bowl.

2  Add the onion and garlic to the skillet, and cook in the same manner, charring evenly on all sides, about 3 minutes. Transfer to the bowl.

3  Add the guajillo and chiles de árbol, and lightly toast, turning them often to ensure even toasting, about 30 to 40 seconds. Be careful not to burn these chiles or the salsa will have a bitter flavor. They only need a light toast.

4  Transfer 2 tomatoes to a blender along with the chile guajillo, chiles de árbol, and the salt. Blend on high into a smooth puree, about 1 minute. Add the rest of the tomatoes, the jalapeños, the onion, and the lime juice. Blend on medium to your desired consistency. I prefer mine to have a medium texture with a bit of runniness.

5  Serve. Store any leftovers in an airtight container in the refrigerator for up to 5 days.

## COOKING NOTES

*If your skillet isn't big enough, you can cook the vegetables in batches until everything is charred.*

# SALSA TUÉTANO

**PREP TIME**
2 minutes

**COOK TIME**
30 minutes

**MAKES**
about 3½ cups

Tuétano (bone marrow) has a silky texture and drops a rich flavor bomb of umami onto whatever you serve it with. It also brings vitamins, minerals, and essential fatty acids to the table. I like to call it "beefy butter" because tuétano is commonly used to top grilled rib eyes or even spread over fresh tortillas in place of butter. It is also exceptionally delicious when added to a roasted salsa and creates a very unique flavor. In this recipe, the ingredients are fire roasted, but you can achieve a similar result by oven roasting them.

3 (6-inch/15cm) beef marrow bones, split in half lengthwise

1 tsp olive or vegetable oil

1¼ tsp salt, divided

3 serrano chiles

5 Roma tomatoes

½ medium white onion

2 garlic cloves

1 bunch of chopped fresh cilantro

Juice of 1 lime

1  Preheat the grill (or the oven) to 300°F (150°C).

2  Lightly brush the marrow bones with oil, and season all over with ¼ teaspoon of salt.

3  Place the bones onto the grill, marrow side down. (If preparing in the oven, place the marrow side up and do not flip.) Add the serranos, tomatoes, onion, and garlic to the grill, and roast, turning often to evenly develop char, about 15 minutes.

4  Remove the vegetables from the heat, and set aside to cool for 5 minutes.

5  Flip over the bones, marrow side up, and cook until the bone marrow is fully cooked and has a very soft, almost runny texture with plenty of char developed, about 15 to 20 minutes.

6  Add the roasted vegetables, cilantro, lime juice, and the remaining 1 teaspoon of salt to a blender, and blend on medium until your desired consistency, about 1 minute.

7  Pour the salsa into a bowl. Scrape the marrow from the bones into the salsa, and mix well with a fork. (This salsa is best eaten fresh the day it's made.)

## COOKING NOTES

*The most popular bones to use for this recipe are beef shank bones. These usually can be found at Mexican or Hispanic grocery stores. If you don't see them, you can ask to speak to a butcher at your grocery store. They might be able to get you some.*

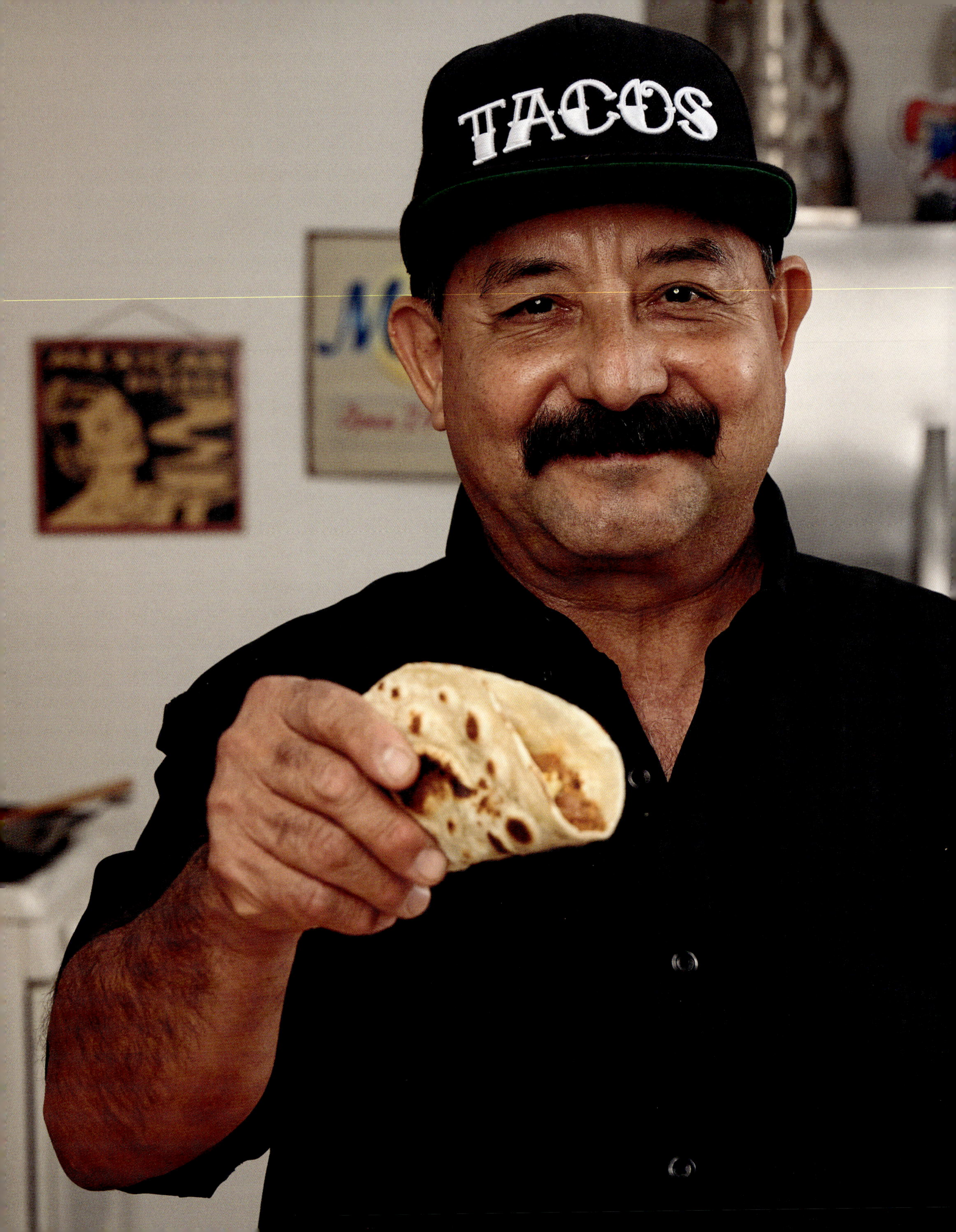
TACOS

# 3

# BREAKFAST

# CON HUEVOS–PAPAS

My kids grew up loving this dish. Two simple ingredients, papas (potatoes) and eggs (huevos), come together and make for a hearty bite. Although there are many ways to fry the potatoes, this recipe uses my favorite technique. You can use a different approach if you like and still have an awesome recipe that can be modified and taken in many different directions. I do recommend enjoying at least one taco simply with papas con huevos at least once a week.

★ ★ ★

2½ cups plus 1 tsp vegetable or another neutral oil

1 large russet potato, peeled, rinsed, and diced into ½-inch (1.25cm) cubes

3 large eggs

¼ tsp salt

1 dash of black pepper

1 garlic clove

1 tbsp salted butter

1  Add 2½ cups of oil to a large pot set over medium-high heat. Heat the oil to 350°F (180°C).

2  Carefully and slowly drop the potatoes into the boiling oil. Use a slotted spoon or spider strainer to stir and ensure the potatoes do not stick together.

3  While the potatoes fry, crack the eggs into a small bowl, add the salt and pepper, and whisk with a fork.

4  After the potatoes have been frying for 2 minutes, add the garlic and fry for 2 minutes. Remove the potatoes and garlic from the oil when the potatoes reach the golden-brown color you prefer, about 5 minutes.

5  Set a 10-inch (25.5cm) skillet over medium heat, and add the remaining 1 teaspoon of oil and the butter.

6  Pour the eggs into the skillet, and immediately start stirring. Cook, stirring, for 30 seconds.

7  Add the potatoes and garlic to the eggs, and stir to ensure the eggs evenly coat the potatoes as much as possible. Turn off the heat and remove the skillet from the burner. The carry-over heat will continue to cook the eggs for another few minutes.

8  Serve immediately with warm tortillas and refried beans on the side.

## PRO TIPS

*Warm a flour tortilla; and add refried beans, American cheese, a whole slice of bacon, and some papas con huevos inside; and you've got the legendary Q-taco of the Rio Grande Valley.*

# CON HUEVOS—BACON

**PREP TIME**
5 minutes

**COOK TIME**
15 minutes

**SERVES**
4

Bacon and eggs are probably the most iconic, simple, and delicious breakfast, and bacon is great for any meal—I hear some people even put it in dessert! For me, thick-cut bacon scrambled into eggs is a thing of beauty, especially when folded into a tortilla and topped with a healthy serving of salsa.

★ ★ ★

4 strips thick-cut bacon, cut into ½-inch (1.25cm) slices
1 tbsp salted butter

6 large eggs
1 dash of salt (optional)

1 dash of black pepper
1 dash of granulated garlic

1  Heat a 10-inch (25.5cm) skillet over medium-low heat. When the skillet is hot, add the bacon and cover. (I like to use a skillet with a lid so the steam encourages faster and more even cooking.) Uncover and stir the bacon every couple minutes. The bacon will release water and render oil in the first few minutes. Have patience here, and you will be rewarded with perfectly cooked bacon, about 6 to 8 minutes. Shut the heat off when the bacon is fully cooked.

2  Drain most of the bacon grease from the skillet and then add the butter. Set the skillet back over medium-low heat.

3  Crack the eggs into a small bowl and whisk with a fork. Add the salt (if using), pepper, and granulated garlic, and whisk to incorporate.

4  When the butter is melted, add the eggs to the skillet. Begin stirring to fully incorporate the bacon with the eggs. Continue cooking for about 3 to 4 minutes or until the eggs are cooked to your preference.

## COOKING NOTES

*You can add diced white onions, Roma tomatoes, and jalapeños to this dish—or any Mexican scramble—for what we in the Rio Grande Valley call an "à la mexicana" dish, which packs a whole other level of flavor and deliciousness.*

# CON HUEVOS—CHORIZO

**PREP TIME**
5 minutes

**COOK TIME**
12 minutes

**SERVES**
4

If bacon is the all-American breakfast, chorizo is the all-Mexican/Tex-Mex all-star. This finely ground pork sausage is thoroughly seasoned with chili pepper, garlic, paprika, salt, and herbs. For breakfast, chorizo makes several appearances with potatoes and nopales, and some taquerias serve it estilo campechano, which is sautéed with bistec and chicharrónes (pork rinds). Back to breakfast though, chorizo is an essential ingredient that, due to its high seasoning content, when it is scrambled with eggs, doesn't need much more than a warm tortilla and salsa for a filling meal.

2 tsp cooking oil or lard
8 oz (225g) pork or beef chorizo

4 large eggs
¼ tsp salt
1 dash of granulated garlic

1 dash of black pepper
1 tbsp salted butter

1 Heat a 10-inch (25.5cm) skillet over medium heat, and add the oil. When the oil is hot, add the chorizo, and cook, stirring often and breaking it into smaller and smaller chunks, until browned, up to about 7 minutes. (Chorizo doesn't need to be seared, and too much high heat can cause sticking, so keep it on medium until it is cooked.)

2 While the chorizo is cooking, crack the eggs into a small bowl and whisk with a fork. Add the salt, granulated garlic, and pepper to the eggs and continue to beat.

3 Add the butter to the chorizo, stir well, and cook for another minute.

4 Pour the eggs into the skillet with the chorizo, and stir to incorporate. Continue cooking until the eggs are cooked to your preference, about 3 or 4 minutes.

5 Serve alongside your favorite style of potatoes and refried beans. I love to scoop these up with a flour tortilla.

# CON HUEVOS—NOPALES

Nopales are an overlooked superfood. Nopales are the pads of the prickly pear cactus, the official plant of Texas. Nopales have a unique, tangy flavor; a slightly crunchy texture; and a beautiful green color. In addition to their health benefits, such as their high antioxidant content and anti-inflammatory effects, they're also resilient, surviving in some of the toughest conditions and making them a part of the fabric of Mexican cuisine.

★ ★ ★

### NOPALES

2 tbsp cooking oil, divided

3 cups diced and rinsed nopales (you can purchase them diced or dice your own)

⅓ medium white onion, diced

1 Roma tomato, diced

1 tbsp chili powder

1 tsp granulated garlic

½ tsp ground cumin

½ tsp salt

1 dash of black pepper

¼ cup fresh cilantro, roughly chopped

Juice of ½ lime or lemon

### SCRAMBLE

½ tbsp salted butter

4 large eggs

1 To make the nopales, heat a 12-inch (30.5cm) skillet over medium heat, and add 1 tablespoon of oil. When the oil is hot, add the nopales and sauté, stirring constantly, for 5 minutes. A slimy texture will begin to come out of the nopales; continue cooking and stirring, and this will evaporate.

2 After 2 minutes, add the onion and tomato and continue stirring.

3 At the 5-minute mark, add ½ cup water and reduce the heat to medium-low to create a low simmer. Add the chili powder, granulated garlic, cumin, salt, and pepper, and stir to incorporate. Cover and simmer for 10 minutes.

4 Uncover, add the cilantro and lime juice, and simmer for 5 minutes.

5 You can enjoy the nopales at this point, which is essentially a guiso (stew) that can be served with fresh or refried beans and Mexican rice, but to continue making the nopales con huevos, heat a 10-inch (25.5cm) skillet over medium heat and add the remaining 1 tablespoon of oil. When the oil is hot, strain and add as much of the prepared nopales as you would like to the skillet. I recommend using at least half.

6 Add the butter, and stir to incorporate in the nopales.

7 Crack the eggs into a small bowl, and whisk with a fork. Add the eggs to the skillet, and cook, stirring, until the eggs reach your desired doneness.

8 Serve with corn tortillas and fresh salsa.

# BARBACOA ESPECIAL

**PREP TIME**
10 minutes

**COOK TIME**
6 to 8 hours

**SERVES**
8

Barbacoa translates as "barbecue," and this version has been around since before it was a thing in Central Texas. The farther south of the border you travel, the more likely you are to find it. The recipe originated with lamb, but in northern Mexico and southern Texas, it evolved to use "cabezas," or whole cow heads, seasoned and buried in a pozo (hole) with hot coals to steam overnight. Now you can find barbacoa in two ways in South Texas: the traditional cachete (cheek meat) only, and "especial," which combines cachete and lengua (tongue) for a heartier bite. Don't be fooled by the chuck roast or other cuts marketed as barbacoa. This recipe is easy to make and great for any meal of the day. It's also commonly served alongside menudo for after-parties and tornabodas.

1 × 1 or 2 lb (450g or 1kg) beef tongue

3 lb (1.35kg) cheek meat

2 tsp salt

½ tsp black pepper

3 garlic cloves

½ medium white onion, plus ½ medium white onion, diced, for garnish

1 bay leaf

Corn or flour tortillas

1 bunch of fresh cilantro, chopped, for garnish

Pico de Gallo (page 34), or your favorite salsa

1   Add the whole, untrimmed tongue (lengua) to the slow cooker. (There's no need to peel the tongue. The skin will fall right off after it's cooked.)

2   Trim some of the excessive fat off of the cheek meat (cachete). (This is not entirely necessary, but I like to do it to preserve my preferred meat-to-grease ratio.) Add the trimmed meat to a 7-quart (6.5-liter) slow cooker.

3   Add the salt, pepper, garlic, ½ onion, and bay leaf to the slow cooker, and pour in ½ cup of water. Cover, and cook on high for 4 hours.

4   At the 4-hour mark, check the meat and rotate and flip it to ensure even cooking. Cover and cook for another 2 hours on high.

5   By this time, the meat should be well done and falling apart. If the lengua is still too firm, cook it for 2 more hours with the cachete. You won't overcook either in that time.

6   When ready to serve, remove the meat from the slow cooker. Chop the cachete or pull it apart with your hands. Peel off the lengua skin and discard, then slice and chop the lengua. Add the lengua to the cachete, and toss to incorporate.

7   To serve, fill a tortilla with the delicious barbacoa especial, garnish with cilantro and diced onion, and top with Pico de Gallo or your favorite salsa. Serve alongside traditional sides like fried beans or menudo.

# CHORIPAPAS

With so many delicious breakfast recipes in Mexican cooking, chorizo con papas, aka choripapas, is a favorite for a hearty dish that is absolutely delicious. Using enough potatoes and chorizo is key so you have plenty to fill your plates and tacos. For an extra-delicious flavor, you can add 2 garlic cloves to the frying oil with the potatoes and ¼ of a small white onion when you fry the chorizo. This dish is commonly served with refried beans and looks and tastes great when topped with a bright green jalapeño-based salsa like Salsa Verde—Base (page 40).

2½ cups canola or vegetable oil

1 large russet potato (about 1 lb/450g), peeled, rinsed, and diced into ½-inch (1.25cm) cubes

8 oz (225g) your favorite chorizo

¼ tsp salt

1 dash of black pepper

⅛ tsp granulated garlic

1   Heat a medium saucepan over medium heat. Add the oil, and heat to 350°F (180°C). When the oil is hot, very carefully add the potatoes and stir immediately with a slotted spoon or spider strainer so the potatoes do not stick. Continue to occasionally stir throughout the frying process, every 2 minutes or so.

2   Around the 3- to 4-minute mark, the potatoes will begin to turn a golden-brown color around the edges and start to float. Remove them from the oil at this time and transfer to a bowl.

3   Heat a 12-inch (30.5cm) skillet over medium heat, and add 2 teaspoons of the potato frying oil. When the oil is hot, add the chorizo and break into small pieces. When the chorizo is halfway cooked, about 2 or 3 minutes, add the potatoes to the skillet and cook, stirring, for 3 minutes to evenly incorporate the chorizo with the potatoes.

4   Add the salt, pepper, and granulated garlic, and stir for 2 minutes to incorporate.

5   Serve immediately.

## COOKING NOTES

*Be sure the pot is large enough to cook all the potatoes at once or commit to two batches. Also be sure the pot is no more than half full with oil because the level will rise when you add potatoes and begin frying.*

PREP TIME
10 minutes

COOK TIME
10 minutes

SERVES
4

# CHICHARRÓN EN SALSA VERDE

Chicharrón comes in a few variations: cracklings, the most common type you can buy in the chip section of grocery stores; chicharrón de cuero (with skin and a little fat); and my favorite, chicharrón con carnita (with meat). The latter two can be found in most Mexican or Hispanic food stores and markets ready to go into this recipe. Use whichever is available to you, and if possible, I recommend trying each of these chicharrónes at least once to find your favorite.

★ ★ ★

1 tbsp cooking oil

3 cups chicharrón con carnita, cut into ½- to 1-inch (1.25–2.5cm) cubes

1 cup Salsa Verde—Tomatillos (page 42)

1   Heat a 12-inch (30.5cm) skillet over medium heat, and add the oil. When the oil is hot, add the chicharrón con carnita and cook, stirring, for 3 minutes. (These are already cooked, so you just need to warm them and toast them a bit to soften them.)

2   After 3 minutes, add the Salsa Verde—Tomatillos to the pan and stir to incorporate the chicharrónes evenly in the salsa. Cover the pan, reduce the heat to low, and simmer the chicharrón for 5 minutes. If you prefer your chicharrónes even softer, continue simmering for up to an additional 5 minutes.

3   Serve immediately. You can enjoy the chicharrón in a taco all on its own or with a slather of beans, or you can cook a pan of scrambled eggs for a heftier pairing.

## COOKING NOTES

*For a whole different eating experience and flavor, you can substitute Salsa Roja—Boiled (page 38) for the Salsa Verde—Tomatillos.*

*To make a pan of scrambled eggs, crack 4 large eggs into a bowl and whisk. While the chicharrón is simmering, heat a medium skillet over medium heat, and add 1 tablespoon salted butter. When the butter is melted, add the eggs and begin to stir. Season with a dash of salt and pepper, and cook until your desired doneness for scrambled eggs.*

# CHILAQUILES ROJOS

The first time I had chilaquiles was in the early 1980s, when I was traveling to Mexico City for work. The quartered and fried corn tortillas covered in salsa left their mark on me, but it would be decades before I began to make them, mostly due to the disproportional popularity of migas in my region. There are so many ways to garnish and top this dish. This recipe is the ArnieTex version, which focuses on my favorite chiles and ingredients.

★ ★ ★

**TOTOPOS**
4 cups cooking oil
9 corn tortillas, cut in quarters
Pinch of salt

**SALSA**
2 chiles guajillo
1 chile puya
3 chiles de árbol
5 Roma tomatoes

½ medium white onion
2 garlic cloves
1 tsp salt
½ tsp black pepper
1 tbsp cooking oil

1 Heat a large saucepan over medium heat to 350°F (180°C), and add the 4 cups cooking oil. When the oil is hot, add the tortillas and fry, stirring often, until golden brown, about 2 minutes. Remove the tortillas from the oil, and place on a wire rack to cool.

2 Lightly season the totopos with salt.

3 To make the salsa, set a medium saucepan of water over medium-high heat and bring to a boil. Add the chiles guajillo, chile puya, chiles de árbol, tomato, onion, and garlic, and boil until all the vegetables are soft, about 10 minutes. Turn off the heat, let cool for 5 minutes, then transfer the cooked vegetables to a blender.

4 Add the salt and pepper to the blender, and blend on high until smooth, about 2 minutes.

5 Add 1 tablespoon cooking oil to a 12-inch (30.5cm) skillet, and set over medium heat. When the oil is hot, add the salsa and bring to a low simmer.

6 Add the totopos to the salsa, and stir quickly until the salsa completely covers the totopos.

7 Serve immediately with your favorite toppings.

## COOKING NOTES

*For toppings, I recommend 2 over-easy eggs, ¼ of sliced avocado, a sprinkle of queso fresco, a drizzle of Mexican crema, and sliced red onions and diced cilantro on top. This is also great served with serrano Chile Toreados (page 63). Or for a fun bite, scoop up plenty of chilaquiles into a flour tortilla for an awesome taco.*

# MIGAS

**PREP TIME**
5 minutes

**COOK TIME**
10 minutes

**SERVES**
4

Migas is another delicious fried corn tortilla recipe, similar to but not to be confused with chilaquiles, especially because this is my wife Terry's favorite breakfast. We like to use yellow corn tortillas for their familiar flavor. The key here is to add the chips to the eggs at just the right time so you preserve the crunchy texture among the fluffy egg.

1½ cups cooking oil

5 corn tortillas, cut into 1-inch (2.5cm) squares

1 tbsp salted butter

5 large eggs

¼ tsp salt

1 dash of black pepper

1 pinch of granulated garlic

Grated American cheese (optional)

1 Heat a 3-quart (2.8-liter) saucier pan, deep enough so the oil is below the halfway point, over medium-high heat, and add the oil. When the oil is hot (350°F/180°C), add half of the tortillas and fry for 2 or 3 minutes. When they are floating and golden brown, remove them from the oil immediately and set on a plate to cool. Repeat with the second batch of tortillas.

2 Set a 10-inch (25.5cm) skillet over medium heat and add the butter.

3 While the butter melts, crack the eggs into a small bowl; season with the salt, pepper, and granulated garlic; and whisk with a fork.

4 When the butter has melted, add the eggs to the pan and stir. When the eggs are halfway cooked, about 1 or 2 minutes, add the crispy tortilla chips and stir gently to incorporate into the eggs.

5 Turn off the heat, and remove the pan from the heat while the eggs finish cooking to your desired doneness.

6 Sprinkle with American cheese (if using), and serve immediately. Try it alongside refried beans, fried potatoes, and your favorite salsa.

## COOKING NOTES

*To make cutting the tortillas easier, stack them and cut them all at once. Also, I suggest frying the tortillas in two batches to encourage an even, crispy texture and finish.*

*Terry prefers to eat a plate of migas and use her tortillas as a utensil. I prefer to load up mine into a flour tortilla and top it with grated Longhorn cheddar cheese. However you choose to eat it, it'll be delicious.*

# MACHACADO À LA MEXICANA

Machaca means "crushed," and in this recipe, the dried beef is pounded into a fine and somewhat stringy texture. In South Texas, this is more commonly known as machacado. (Some mistakenly refer to this as beef jerky–like, but it's not.) This is an absolute staple in North Mexico, South Texas, and along the border, and it's a traditional Norteño breakfast. Its delicious beefy taste and unique texture make it a perfect accompaniment to scrambled eggs. This recipe is "à la mexicana," with onions, tomatoes, and chiles, but you can omit those ingredients if you want a more pronounced meat flavor. One of my favorite things about this recipe is how fast and easy it is to cook.

★ ★ ★

2 tbsp cooking oil
4 oz (115g) machaca
1 tbsp salted butter

¼ white onion, diced
1 Roma tomato, diced

1 jalapeño, diced
5 large eggs

1 Heat a 12-inch (30.5cm) skillet over medium-high heat, and add the oil. When the oil is hot, add the machaca and stir for 1 minute to develop a slight char on the meat.

2 Add the butter, and cook, stirring, until the meat is evenly coated in the butter, about 2 minutes.

3 Add the onion, tomato, and jalapeño to the skillet, and cook, stirring to incorporate them with the machaca, for 2 minutes.

4 Crack the eggs into a small bowl, and whisk with a fork. Pour the eggs into the skillet, and cook, stirring, until the eggs are your desired doneness.

5 Serve immediately with tortillas and refried beans. For heat, add your favorite salsa or a serrano Chile Toreados (page 63).

# HUEVOS RANCHEROS

**PREP TIME**
5 minutes

**COOK TIME**
5 minutes

**SERVES**
2

There are so many variations on this recipe, but I prefer my huevos rancheros served how I remember eating them when I was growing up: basted and completely smothered in a ranchera sauce. You can use Salsa Roja–Ranchera (page 37) for this recipe. Rather than flipping over-easy eggs, I prefer to cook the eggs in a nonstick pan, cover with a lid, and baste them to perfection.

1 tbsp salted butter

2 large eggs

1 dash of salt

1 dash of black pepper

1 pinch of granulated garlic

½ cup warm Salsa Roja—Ranchera (page 37)

1  Heat a 10-inch (25.5cm) nonstick skillet over medium heat, and add the butter.

2  While the butter melts, carefully crack the eggs into a small bowl.

3  When the butter is fully melted, add the eggs to the pan, cover with a lid, and steam for 1 minute.

4  Check the eggs at the 1-minute mark. As soon as the whites start to look set and are halfway cooked, pour 2 teaspoons of water on the side of the pan, away from the eggs, and place the lid back on. Steam for 30 seconds.

5  Check the eggs to see if they are at your desired doneness. If not, put the lid back on and steam for 30 more seconds.

6  Remove the lid, and season the eggs with the salt, pepper, and granulated garlic.

7  When the eggs are cooked to your preference, slide them onto a plate, smother them with the warm Salsa Roja—Ranchera, and serve.

## PRO TIPS

*This recipe is delicious when served with loose refried beans. For the full experience, tear some tortillas into small pieces and use them as utensils. That's the good stuff right there, sopping up all the runny egg, salsa, and beans.*

# HUEVOS DIVORCIADOS

This is a slight evolution on huevos rancheros. Literally translated as "divorced eggs," this recipe demonstrates its moniker by separating two eggs between a row of refried beans and fried potatoes. One egg is topped with a salsa verde and the other with a salsa roja. The dish is easy to customize, with some serving the eggs sunny-side up with the yolk exposed, others opting to smother the eggs with salsa, and still others serving the eggs atop fresh fried tostadas for an added crunch. Have fun with this recipe.

1 tbsp salted butter

2 large eggs

1 dash of salt

1 dash of black pepper

1 pinch of granulated garlic

Refried Beans—Three Ways, stage 2 (page 205)

Warm fried potatoes

½ cup warm Salsa Roja—Ranchera (page 37)

½ cup warm Salsa Verde—Tomatillos (page 42)

1   Set a 12-inch (30.5cm) nonstick skillet over medium heat, and add the butter.

2   While the butter melts, carefully crack the eggs into a small bowl.

3   When the butter is fully melted, add the eggs to the pan, cover with a lid, and steam for 1 minute.

4   Check the eggs at the 1-minute mark. As soon as the whites start to look set and are halfway cooked, pour 2 teaspoons of water on the side of the pan, away from the eggs, and place the lid back on. Steam until just sunny-side up, about 30 seconds.

5   Check the eggs with a fork to see if they're done. If not, put the lid back on and steam for 30 more seconds.

6   Remove the lid, and season the eggs with salt, pepper, and granulated garlic.

7   Place a serving of refried beans in the center of a plate, followed by a serving of potatoes. Slide 1 egg onto one side of the plate and the other egg onto the opposite side. Smother 1 egg in the warm Salsa Roja—Ranchera and the other in the warm Salsa Verde—Tomatillos, and serve.

## COOKING NOTES

*You can use any fried potatoes you like, or try the potato-cooking method used in Con Huevos—Papas (page 68). For presentation purposes, you can keep the eggs completely separate as they steam for a nice plating later. If the whites run together, separate them using a wooden spoon or spatula prior to flipping or plating.*

# COSTRA DE QUESO

Cheese is one of the most-used ingredients in breakfast tacos, especially in Texas. You can lay it on the bottom so it melts beneath your filling or sprinkle it on top for a fresh-grated flavor. There's also a third way to incorporate cheese into tacos: costra style. Costra, meaning "crust," can be a textural addition to your tortilla or the tortilla itself. It just takes the right heat, some attention, and patience.

10 oz (285g) cold Oaxaca or
  cheddar cheese

1 Remove the cheese from the refrigerator and immediately grate it.

2 Heat a griddle, saucepan, or skillet over medium-low heat. Add ¼ of the cheese to the pan, and evenly spread it out to a tight, semiflat circular shape.

3 Cook the cheese until the edges start to turn golden brown, about 3 minutes. As the cheese melts, it will begin to bubble and release moisture and oil.

4 After about 3 minutes, slowly begin to slide a spatula underneath the edges of the cheese, all the way around, to see if it has crisped up evenly. The costra is ready when it slides around easily in the pan.

5 Add your filling of choice directly on top of the cheese and then fold it closed. Or place a warm tortilla directly on top of the melted cheese, flip it over so the tortilla side is down, remove the pan from the heat, and fill the costra with your choice of ingredients, like you would with a normal taco. This method brings a crunchy, cheesy layer at the bottom of your taco.

## PRO TIPS

*A nonstick pan works best for this recipe. You also can add a light layer of cooking spray or oil to the pan before cooking to help the cheese not stick.*

*Essentially any cheese works well in this recipe. Use your favorite, or experiment with Chihuahua, Monterey Jack, mozzarella, Gouda, asadero, or Manchego.*

# 4
# TAQUERIA EL ARNIE

# EASY AL PASTOR TACOS

**PREP TIME**
15 minutes

**COOK TIME**
20 minutes

**SERVES**
3 or 4

Nearly every taqueria across the world has a tacos al pastor recipe that's a fan favorite, and for good reason. The adobo sauce the pork marinates in overnight packs a deep, complex, yet bright flavor, and the slow roast on a trompo (vertical rotisserie) cooks the pork until it's tender and moist. This easy version allows you to skip the trompo and overnight marinade and whip up these mouthwatering tacos just in time for any occasion.

1 tbsp pork lard or cooking oil

2 lb (1kg) pork butt or pork roast, diced

1½ cups Al Pastor Adobo (page 59)

12 small taco-style corn tortillas, warmed

½ cup roughly chopped fresh cilantro

1 cup small diced white onion

1 cup small diced pineapple

2 limes, cut into quarters

1   Heat a 12-inch (30.5cm) skillet over medium heat, and add the lard. When the lard is hot, add the pork, and spread it to an even layer. As it starts to sear, stir frequently so the pork cooks on all sides. Cover the pan and cook for 10 minutes, uncovering and stirring every 2 or 3 minutes to ensure even cooking.

2   Add the Al Pastor Adobo, and stir well. Reduce the heat to medium, cover, and cook for 5 minutes. Every 2 minutes, uncover, stir, and recover.

3   Uncover the pan, and cook for 5 more minutes. (This will allow the excess water to evaporate while the adobo fully sets into the meat.) Turn off the heat when your desired consistency is reached.

4   To warm the tortillas, add 1 to 2 tablespoons of cooking oil to a large skillet set over medium heat. Lay 2 to 4 tortillas in the pan for 5 to 10 seconds, then flip and allow to warm for 5 to 10 seconds more. Add more oil as needed. Transfer to a plate and repeat until all the tortillas are warmed.

5   Add 2 to 3 tablespoons of the easy al pastor to each warm tortilla. Top with cilantro, onion, and pineapple, and serve with limes on the side.

# GRINGAS

Gringas translates as "anglo women," and one of the legends behind these tacos is that a Mexican man traveled north to the United States, only to have his heart broken by his anglo girlfriend. When he returned home, he invented these tacos and called them "gringas" in memory of love lost. I don't know about all that, but I do know this is a delicious twist on tacos al pastor. Serve these either in a single flour tortilla folded over or sincronizada (sandwich) style between two flour tortillas. I recommend making these at the same time as tacos al pastor or the next day using the leftovers.

★ ★ ★

4 flour tortillas
2 cups shredded Oaxaca cheese

1½ lb (680g) cooked Easy al Pastor Tacos pork (page 92)
1 cup diced pineapple

1 cup diced white onion
Fresh cilantro
Lime wedges

1   Heat a griddle over medium heat. Add a flour tortilla, warm it for 1 minute, and flip it over. Sprinkle on ¼ cup Oaxaca, add ¼ cup Easy al Pastor pork, and top with pineapple, diced onion, and cilantro.

2   Fold the tortilla in half, and toast, flipping often to avoid burning, until the cheese is melted, about 3 minutes. Repeat with the remaining ingredients.

3   Serve with lime wedges.

# CRISPY TACOS

**PREP TIME**
5 minutes

**COOK TIME**
20 minutes

**SERVES**
4

These tacos were one of my favorite things my mom would cook when I was a kid. The crunchy taco shell, seasoned beef, and fresh toppings just made for a big bite of flavor. Crispy tacos are also a staple in Mexican American cooking and Tex-Mex restaurants.

1 tsp cooking oil

1 tbsp finely diced white onion, or 1 tsp onion powder

1 lb (450g) ground beef

½ tsp salt

1 dash of black pepper

1 garlic clove, minced, or ½ tsp granulated garlic

**TACO SHELLS**

3 cups cooking oil

12 corn tortillas

**OPTIONAL TOPPINGS**

⅓ cup chopped iceberg lettuce

1 cup diced Roma tomatoes

1 cup shredded American cheese

1 large avocado, peeled, pitted, and sliced

Your favorite hot sauce

1  Heat a 12-inch (30.5cm) skillet over medium heat, and add 1 teaspoon of oil. When the oil is hot, add the onions and ground beef, and begin to brown the meat, stirring continuously.

2  After 3 minutes, add the salt, pepper, and garlic. Reduce the heat to medium-low, and stir to incorporate. Cover and cook for 5 minutes.

3  Remove the pan from the heat, cover, and set aside.

4  In a separate 12-inch (30.5cm) skillet, heat 3 cups of oil to 300°F (150°C). Using tongs and a spatula, add the tortillas to the oil, one at a time, and immediately flip them over and then fold them in half.

5  Fry until the tortilla develops a golden-brown color, 30 to 40 seconds or up to 1 minute, flipping once at the halfway mark. To encourage a taco-shell shape, use the tongs or spatula to hold the tortilla open slightly. When the tortilla is fully crispy, transfer it to a cooling rack or a paper towel–lined plate to drain, and repeat with the remaining tortillas.

6  Fill the crunchy taco shells with 2 to 3 tablespoons of the ground beef and your toppings of choice, and serve.

## COOKING NOTES

*When cooking the tortillas, start with only one at a time. After you have mastered this process, you may be able to cook up to three at a time, depending on the size of your pan.*

# BAJA FISH _AND_ SHRIMP TACOS

This recipe has origins on the coasts of Baja California, Mexico, and it has so much goodness going on. Fold all that up into a warm corn tortilla, and you have one of the most iconic and delicious tacos in the world.

★ ★ ★

5 cups cooking oil

2 lb (1kg) halibut fish, sliced

2 lb (1kg) large shrimp, deveined and rinsed

10 corn tortillas

8 lime wedges

### CHIPOTLE SAUCE

¾ cup mayonnaise

3 tbsp lime juice

2 canned chipotles in adobo sauce

1 tbsp adobo sauce from the can

1 tbsp apple cider vinegar

1 tbsp Mexican crema

½ tsp chili powder

1 large garlic clove, roughly chopped

¼ tsp salt

### SLAW

4 cups cabbage, finely sliced

2 tbsp minced white onion

½ cup chopped fresh cilantro

1 tbsp apple cider vinegar

3 tbsp lime juice

¼ cup mayonnaise

½ tsp salt

### BEER BATTER

¼ tsp ground cumin

1½ tsp salt

½ tsp black pepper

1 tsp chili powder

¾ tsp granulated garlic

1 tsp baking powder

1 cup all-purpose flour

8 oz (236ml) beer, plus more as needed

1  To make the chipotle sauce, add all the chipotle sauce ingredients to a blender, and blend until smooth and creamy. If the texture is too thick, drizzle in 1 tablespoon of water at a time and blend again until the desired consistency is reached. Transfer to a squeeze bottle or a small bowl, and place in the refrigerator.

2  To make the slaw, add all the slaw ingredients to a large bowl, and mix well. Cover and place in the refrigerator.

3  To make the beer batter, add the cumin, salt, pepper, chili powder, granulated garlic, and baking powder to another large bowl, and mix well. Add the flour, and mix well again. Pour in the beer, and stir to combine. If the batter is too thick, add a few more ounces of beer. (You can use up to 12 ounces [350ml] total in the batter.)

4  Add the oil to a deep saucepan, set over medium-high heat, and heat to 350°F (180°C). Place the halibut slices in the batter one at a time, turn to coat evenly, and transfer directly to the hot oil, adding the fish to the oil slowly to avoid splattering. You can fry 3 or 4 pieces at a time; any more at once risks cooling the oil too much. Fry the fish until it floats for 15 to 20 seconds, about 3 or 4 minutes. Check the fish with a meat thermometer; it should be between 145°F and 150°F (63°C and 66°C) in the thickest part. Transfer the cooked fish to a cooling rack or a paper towel–lined plate to drain. Repeat with the remaining fish and then the shrimp.

5  Set a comal or a large skillet over medium heat, and warm the tortillas, flipping until both sides are cooked, about 3 minutes. Transfer the warm tortillas to a plate.

6  Top the tortillas with 1 piece of fried halibut and/or 2 or 3 shrimp, ⅛ cup slaw, a drizzle of the chipotle sauce, and a squeeze of lime, and serve.

# TORTAS DE DESHEBRADA

**PREP TIME**
15 minutes

**COOK TIME**
5 hours

**SERVES**
3

A torta is a sandwich that draws inspiration from both French baking and Spanish cuisine with an authentic Mexican expression. Like any other sandwich, the ways this recipe can be customized are infinite. This version is similar to what you would find at a taqueria in Texas's Rio Grande Valley and great served alongside pickled jalapeños or your favorite salsa.

3 large bolillo breads

6 tbsp Refried Beans—Three Ways, stage 2 (page 205), warmed

¾ cup shredded Oaxaca cheese

3 slices of ham

¾ cup thinly sliced iceberg lettuce

1 Roma tomato, thinly sliced

1 large avocado, peeled, pitted, and mashed

¼ cup Mexican crema

**SAUCE**

2 chiles guajillo, deseeded

5 chiles de árbol, deseeded

2 jalapeños

1 cup diced red bell pepper

3 garlic cloves

5 Roma tomatoes

2 tomatillos

1 medium white onion, quartered

¼ cup diced celery

¼ cup diced carrot

**SEASONINGS**

2 tsp salt

¼ tsp black pepper

½ tsp ground cumin

½ tsp dried oregano

2 tbsp Worcestershire sauce

**CARNE DESHEBRADA**

1 tsp cooking oil

2 lb (1kg) chuck, cut into 2-inch (5cm) pieces

3 cups water or chicken broth

1  To make the sauce, fill an 8-quart (7.8-liter) stockpot half full with water. Add all the sauce ingredients to the stockpot, and set over medium-high heat. Bring to a light boil, and cook for 10 minutes. Transfer the ingredients to a blender.

2  Add the salt, pepper, cumin, oregano, and Worcestershire sauce to the blender, and blend until smooth. Set the sauce aside.

3  To make the carne deshebrada, add the oil to a large skillet, and set over medium-high heat. When the oil is hot, add the chuck and sear on all sides, about 3 to 5 minutes per side. Transfer to a 7-quart (6.5-liter) slow cooker.

4  Add the water or chicken broth to the slow cooker along with 3 cups of the sauce. Cover and cook on high for 4 to 5 hours or until the meat is tender.

5  Transfer the meat to a baking sheet or large plate. Shred using two forks or chop with a heavy knife or cleaver. Return it to the slow cooker to keep warm.

6  Slice the bolillo breads in half so they open like a sandwich. In a 12-inch (30.5cm) skillet or griddle set over medium-low heat, lightly toast both sides of each loaf of bread. Transfer to a plate.

7  On each bottom half of the bolillos, spread 2 tablespoons warm refried beans in an even layer. Top with ¼ cup of Oaxaca. Add 1 slice of ham, ¼ cup of shredded lettuce, 3 tomato slices, and 2 to 4 ounces of carne deshebrada. On each top half of the bolillos, spread 2 tablespoons of avocado and drizzle about 1 tablespoon of Mexican crema on top. Place the top bun over the bottom half, and serve.

# TACOS GOBERNADOR

**PREP TIME**
15 minutes

**COOK TIME**
15 minutes

**SERVES**
4

The governor of Sinaloa, Mexico, was known for loving shrimp. While visiting Mazatlán in 1987, he stopped at a restaurant called Los Arcos, where the chefs surprised him with these very special shrimp-based tacos. Some of the recipe's history is hard to nail down, but one thing is for certain: If you're a fan of shrimp, tacos, or cheese, you'll love these tacos.

1 tsp salt

1 tsp black pepper

1 lb (450g) whole shrimp, heads removed, peeled, deveined, and rinsed

4 tbsp salted butter, divided

⅓ medium white onion, diced

½ chile poblano, diced

1 Roma tomato, diced

2 garlic cloves, minced

12 corn tortillas

1 cup grated Oaxaca cheese

1 bunch of fresh cilantro, chopped

2 limes, cut into wedges

Your favorite salsa

1   Mix the salt and pepper in a small bowl. Set aside.

2   Depending on the size of the shrimp, cut each into two or three pieces about ½ inch (1.25cm) long.

3   Set a 12-inch (30.5cm) skillet over medium heat, and add 2 tablespoons of butter. Add the onions and chile poblano, and sauté for 5 minutes.

4   Increase the heat to medium-high, add the tomatoes and garlic, and sauté for 2 minutes.

5   Add the shrimp. Season lightly with the salt and pepper, and cook, stirring often, until fully cooked, about 3 to 4 minutes. Check the shrimp with a meat thermometer; it should be between 140°F and 145°F (60°C and 63°C) in the thickest part. Turn off the heat.

6   Set another 12-inch (30.5cm) skillet over medium heat, and add the remaining 2 tablespoons of butter. When the butter is melted, add 3 tortillas at a time to the pan. Flip over the tortillas after 20 seconds, add about 1 or 2 tablespoons of Oaxaca to each tortilla, fill with ¼ cup shrimp, and fold over.

7   Toast each side of the folded taco until it's a bit crispy on each side, about 30 to 45 seconds. If you prefer a crispier shell, keep flipping for up to another minute.

8   Serve, garnished with cilantro and lime wedges and your favorite salsa on the side.

# CACHETEADAS

**PREP TIME**
5 minutes

**COOK TIME**
5 minutes

**SERVES**
3

Cacheteada means "slap," and this recipe gets its playful name from the assembly method: A thinly sliced cut of meat is seared on both sides and then "slapped" into a warm tortilla. In 2024, a taqueria in Mexico City was awarded a Michelin star for tacos served in this style. So if you can't make it to Taquería El Califa de León this year, then try this recipe. It can be made on a plancha (griddle), on the grill, or with a heavy-bottom pan like cast iron. This is a great choice for mixing up your taco nights.

1 tsp salt

1 tsp black pepper

9 very thinly sliced rib eyes, skirt steaks, or pork chops

1 tbsp cooking oil

9 corn tortillas, warmed

1 bunch of fresh cilantro, chopped

½ medium white onion, diced

Salsa Verde–Tomatillos (page 42)

1  Mix the salt and pepper in a small bowl.

2  Season the rib eyes all over with the salt and pepper.

3  Heat a griddle over high heat, and add the oil. When the oil is hot, add the rib eyes to the griddle, and allow to quickly sear. After 1 minute, flip over the meat and sear for 1 minute on the other side. Remove from the heat.

4  To warm the tortillas, add 1 to 2 tablespoons of cooking oil to a large skillet set over medium heat. Lay 2 to 4 tortillas in the pan for 5 to 10 seconds, then flip and allow to warm for 5 to 10 seconds more. Add more oil as needed. Transfer to a plate and repeat until all the tortillas are warmed.

5  Top each tortilla with an entire rib eye. Garnish with some cilantro, onion and a drizzle of Salsa Verde—Tomatillos, and serve.

# TACOS DE BISTEC

**PREP TIME**
10 minutes

**COOK TIME**
10 minutes

**SERVES**
4 or 5

The number-one meat for street tacos in South Texas is bistec. Because the word *bistec* is basically a catch-all translation for "beef steak" any cut of beef can be used in these quick tacos, but you'll find finely diced chuck or sirloin used most often. The fine dice allows for extremely fast cooking, making it a go-to choice for taquerias and restaurants.

1 tsp salt

¼ tsp black pepper

1 tsp garlic powder

½ tsp onion powder

2 tbsp cooking oil

2½ lb (1.25kg) thinly sliced chuck, diced

20 small taqueria-style corn tortillas, warmed

½ cup roughly chopped fresh cilantro

1 cup small diced white onion

**CONDIMENTS**

Lime wedges

Salsa Verde—Taqueria (page 43)

Salsa Roja—Taqueria (page 39)

Avocado, peeled, pitted, and sliced

1  Blend the salt, pepper, garlic powder, and onion powder in a small bowl. Set aside.

2  Heat a griddle over high heat, and add the oil. When the oil is hot, add the chuck (bistec), spread it to an even layer, and allow it to develop some sear, 2 or 3 minutes.

3  Season the meat evenly with the seasoning blend, and stir to incorporate. (If your griddle isn't hot enough, excess moisture can develop on the surface. Continue stirring a bit as the moisture evaporates before continuing to the next step.)

4  When the bistec has developed some char, begin to stir quickly and often. The whole cooking process will take only a couple minutes. The meat cooks fast, so be careful not to overcook or it can dry out.

5  Remove the bistec from the griddle, and transfer to a plate to rest for 2 to 3 minutes.

6  To warm the tortillas, add 1 to 2 tablespoons of cooking oil to a large skillet set over medium heat. Lay 2 to 4 tortillas in the pan for 5 to 10 seconds, then flip and allow to warm for 5 to 10 seconds more. Add more oil as needed. Transfer to a plate and repeat until all the tortillas are warmed.

7  Add ¼ cup of bistec to each warm tortilla. Top with cilantro and diced onions, and serve with lime wedges, the salsas, and the avocado slices on the side.

## COOKING NOTES

*To make this a combo meal, serve with a cup of Charro Beans (page 202) and small Papa Asada (page 214).*

# 5

# FAJITA FEST

## COOKING NOTES

*Before adding the steak to the grill, be sure to clean the grill thoroughly. It's tradition in South Texas to finish the cleaning process with half an onion (using tongs to hold an onion half, flat side down, and scrape the grill grates back and forth with the onion) to add an extra note of flavor to the meat—and let the neighbors know what's about to go down! In my family, we serve this by layering some guacamole on a flour tortilla, stuffing the tortilla full with fajitas, and then topping the steak with some fresh Pico de Gallo (page 34).*

# FAJITAS—SKIRT STEAK

**PREP TIME**
10 minutes

**COOK TIME**
5 to 10 minutes

**SERVES**
6 to 8

Skirt steak is the original cut of beef for fajitas. However, this cut often gets a bad rap as a tougher cut. That's because most people buy the *inside* skirt steak and have yet to try the *outside* skirt steak, which is much softer, much more tender, and juicier. Because the outside skirt is in greater demand, it's nearly impossible to find at the butcher shop, as restaurants buy them first. Still, it doesn't hurt to ask your butcher. If all they have is the inside skirt, that's okay, because cooking this cut to delicious perfection is just as easy. For even more added flavor and tenderness, pair this recipe with either the Red Carniceria Marinade (page 60) or the Green Fajita Marinade (page 62).

1 whole strip of skirt steak (usually 2½ to 3 lb/ 1.25 to 1.35kg)

ArnieTex Beef Seasoning Blend (page 25)

Wood chunks or chips (your preferred wood; optional)

8 flour or corn tortillas

1 pinch of salt (optional)

Pico de Gallo (page 34)

Guacamole (page 208)

1   Trim the excess fat and tough membrane from both sides of the skirt steak.

2   Season the skirt steak generously with the ArnieTex Beef Seasoning Blend.

3   Cut the strip with the grain into 2 or 3 even-sized pieces, and set aside to allow the seasoning to set.

4   Prepare a charcoal chimney and your grill with enough fuel to run up to 500°F to 600°F (260°C to 315°C). This is a hot and fast cook. For added smoke and flavor, add the wood chunks (if using) to the coals, ensuring that they are lit and emitting a clear, translucent smoke.

5   Place the skirt steak directly over the hot fire. Cook, flipping every 1 or 2 minutes, and start to develop char. Skirt steaks are thin and can be ready in as soon as 5 to 7 minutes and after only a couple of flips. Check for doneness with a meat thermometer; the meat should be between 130°F and 135°F (55°C and 57°C) for medium. Because inside skirt is a tougher cut, a medium doneness will be more tender.

6   Remove the steak from the grill, loosely wrap in aluminum foil or place in a nonreactive cooking pan, and set aside for 10 minutes. After 5 minutes, flip over the steak so it can start to absorb more of the natural au jus.

7   Place the steak on a clean cutting board, and cut across the grain in ¼- to ⅜-inch (0.5–1cm) strips.

8   Taste a piece. Season with a pinch of salt if needed, and serve with tortillas, Pico de Gallo, and Guacamole.

# FAJITAS—RESTAURANT STYLE

**PREP TIME**
10 minutes plus
1 hour to marinate

**COOK TIME**
10 minutes

**SERVES**
5

We've all had that moment at some point in our lives: it's summertime, and you're at your favorite restaurant, waiting for your meal. First you hear it, then you smell it, and finally you see it—that sizzling platter of fajitas … speeding past you to a table with a happier vibe. You think to yourself, *Why the heck didn't I order fajitas?* With this recipe, you can make restaurant-style fajitas at home. This recipe calls for what is commonly known in South Texas as "Sirloin Fajita," which is technically a bavette steak and also known as "flap meat." This cut of beef is much more tender than skirt steak, thus making it a favorite choice for restaurants to serve.

1½ lb (680g) flap meat

ArnieTex Beef Seasoning Blend (page 25)

2 tbsp cooking oil

1 medium white onion, cut into strips

½ green bell pepper, ribs and seeds removed, and cut into strips

½ yellow bell pepper, ribs and seeds removed, and cut into strips

½ red bell pepper, ribs and seeds removed, and cut into strips

½ cup of chopped fresh cilantro

6 flour or corn tortillas

MommaTex's Mexican Rice (page 207)

Refried Beans—Three Ways, stage 2 (page 205)

Guacamole (page 208)

1  Square up the flap meat around the edges. Slice the meat in half, stack the two pieces, and cut in half again. Then, cutting across the grain, slice the meat into strips ¼ to ⅜ inch (0.5–1cm) thick. Cut the loose pieces of meat (left over from squaring it) into similar-sized strips. Place the strips in a large bowl.

2  Season the meat generously with the ArnieTex Beef Seasoning Blend.

3  Cover the bowl with plastic wrap and place in the refrigerator for at least 1 hour.

4  Heat a 12-inch (30.5cm) skillet or griddle over high heat. This will be a hot and fast cook. Drizzle the oil in the pan, and spread it evenly over the cooking surface. Drop the flap meat in the pan, spread it out evenly, and immediately begin sautéing it.

5  After 4 minutes, add the onion and bell peppers, and cook, stirring quickly, for 2 to 4 more minutes.

6  The flap meat is now at a medium doneness, which is perfect with consideration to the carry-over cooking. Shut off the heat. Sprinkle fresh cilantro over the top, toss once, and transfer to a serving platter.

7  While the meat rests for a few minutes, heat the tortillas in the skillet.

8  Serve with MommaTex's Mexican Rice, Refried Beans—Three Ways, and Guacamole.

## COOKING NOTES

*Instead of the seasoning blend, you can marinate the flap meat with one of the marinade recipes in the Salsas, Sauces, & Marinades chapter.*

# CHICKEN FAJITAS

**PREP TIME**
15 minutes

**COOK TIME**
10 minutes

**SERVES**
3

Historically speaking, there was no such thing as "chicken fajitas" because "fajitas" originally referred to beef skirt steak, specifically the inside skirt steak. As restaurants and meat markets saw the rise in popularity of beef fajitas over time, it just made sense to expand the definition to include chicken. But that doesn't mean this recipe isn't anything short of delicious. My favorite way to make chicken fajitas is with chicken thighs, but you can use the leaner chicken breast if you prefer. The breast is less forgiving, though; it begins to dry out the higher it goes over an internal temperature of 165°F (75°C).

ArnieTex Poultry Seasoning Blend (page 25)

4 boneless, skinless chicken thighs, cut across into ½-inch (1.25cm) strips

2 tbsp cooking oil

1 green bell pepper, ribs and seeds removed, and cut into ¼-inch (6mm) strips

1 red bell pepper, ribs and seeds removed, and cut into ¼-inch (6mm) strips

½ medium white onion, cut into ¼-inch (6mm) strips

6 flour tortillas

1  Liberally apply the ArnieTex Poultry Seasoning Blend to the chicken thighs, covering all sides.

2  Heat a 12-inch (30.5cm) skillet over high heat, and add the oil. When the oil is hot, add the chicken.

3  After about 3 to 5 minutes, and after a bit of char begins to develop on chicken, stir the chicken. Sear for 1 more minute.

4  Add the bell peppers and onion, and cook, stirring, for 5 minutes. Check the chicken for doneness with a meat thermometer; it should be 165°F (75°C) in the thickest part. Remove the skillet from the heat.

5  Warm the tortillas.

6  Fill the tortillas with the chicken and veggies. Serve with MommaTex's Mexican Rice (page 207), Refried Beans—Three Ways (page 205), and Guacamole (page 208).

**6**

# ARNIE'S CAFÉ AND GRILL

# ARNIETEX TEJANO BURGER

**PREP TIME**
10 minutes plus
30 minutes to rest

**COOK TIME**
10 minutes

**SERVES**
2

This is not a skinny little smashburger. Don't get me wrong, I can appreciate the Maillard reaction (the chemical reaction that occurs during the cooking process that causes food to brown and develop texture and flavor) and the delicious, crunchy char you get with smashburgers, but this is South Texas style! You only need one of these big, juicy patties charred and grilled to perfection.

★ ★ ★

1 lb (450g) 80/20 ground beef

¼ cup finely diced white onion

2 tbsp Worcestershire sauce, plus more for drizzling

½ tsp salt

¼ tsp black pepper

¼ tsp granulated garlic

2 slices cheddar cheese (optional)

1 tbsp unsalted butter

2 hamburger buns

**TOPPINGS**

Mustard

Drizzle of hot sauce

¼ cup thinly sliced iceberg lettuce

4 thin tomato slices

10 dill pickle slices

1 Add the ground beef, onion, and 2 tablespoons of Worcestershire sauce to a large bowl, and begin to work it all together using clean hands. When all ingredients are incorporated, form 2 patties.

2 In a small bowl, mix together the salt, pepper, and granulated garlic. Season one side of the patties with half of the salt blend, and set aside for 30 minutes.

3 Preheat the grill to 350°F to 400°F (180°C to 200°C).

4 When the fire is hot, add the patties, seasoning side down, over the coals and let the char start to develop for about 5 minutes. While the patties are cooking, season the top sides of the patties with the remaining salt blend. If flames start to kick up, cover the grill.

5 Flip the patties at the 5-minute mark, and cook for 5 more minutes, covering again only if the flames jump up too much.

6 At the second 5-minute mark, drizzle about ½ teaspoon of Worcestershire sauce over the top of each pattie and immediately top with 1 cheddar slice each (if using). Cover the grill for 1 minute, just to allow the cheese to melt. Remove the patties from the grill, and allow them to rest on a plate for 5 minutes.

7 Lightly butter the hamburger buns and toast them on the grill for 10 to 20 seconds per side.

8 Place the bottom buns on a plate, add 1 patty each, and top with some mustard, hot sauce, lettuce, tomato slices, and pickle slices. Add the top buns, and serve.

## PRO TIPS

*These burgers are best served with homemade fries or potato chips.*

# HAMBURGESA MEXICANA

A simple burger with meat, cheese, and a condiment or two is absolutely delicious. But if we're gonna pile on the toppings, why be shy about it? This Mexican-style burger is popular at most restaurants along the South Texas border because it ups the ante and piles on all the good stuff.

★ ★ ★

1½ lb (680g) 80/20 ground beef
1½ tbsp salt
1½ tbsp black pepper
8 thin strips bacon
2 jalapeños
4 slices American cheese
4 slices ham

4 hamburger buns
½ head iceberg lettuce, thinly chopped
1 Roma tomato, sliced

**MAYO SLATHER**
¼ cup mayonnaise
¼ cup Mexican crema

1 tsp Worcestershire sauce
2 tsp dill pickle juice
1 tsp chili powder
1 garlic clove, minced
Juice of 1 lime
½ avocado, peeled, pitted, and mashed

1 To make the mayo slather, add all the ingredients except the avocado to a medium bowl, and mix well. Mash in the avocado until it is fully incorporated. Set aside.

2 Using clean hands, divide the ground beef into 4 equal portions and form into patties.

3 Mix the salt and pepper in a small bowl. Season one side of the patties with half of the salt and pepper blend, and set aside.

4 In a 12-inch (30.5cm) skillet over medium heat, add the bacon and cook, flipping every 2 or 3 minutes, until fully cooked and crispy, about 6 minutes. Transfer the bacon to a plate.

5 Set a griddle over medium heat. Add the jalapeños to the griddle, not over direct heat, and allow them to blister, about 4 to 6 minutes, rotating every minute for even blistering. When the jalapeños have developed a slight blister on all sides, remove them from the griddle, transfer to the plate, and slice.

6 Add the patties to the skillet, seasoning side down, and cook for 2 minutes. Season the raw side with the remaining salt and pepper blend, flip over the patties, and cook for 1 more minute. Check for doneness with a meat thermometer; the patties should be 160°F (70°C) in the thickest part. Add 1 slice of American cheese to each patty. Transfer the patties to a plate.

7 Add the ham to the skillet, and quickly sear each side for 10 to 15 seconds per side. Transfer to the plate.

8 Spread a light layer of the mayo slather on all sides of the buns, then lightly toast them on the griddle for about 15 seconds per side.

9 Spread both sides of each bun with additional mayo slather. On the bottom buns, place about ¼ of the lettuce, tomato slices, and jalapeño slices. Add 1 patty each, followed by 1 slice of ham and 2 strips of bacon. Add the top buns, and serve.

**PREP TIME**
7 minutes plus
2 hours to
marinate

**COOK TIME**
8 minutes

**SERVES**
2

# STEAK
## [PORTERHOUSE OR T-BONE]

Porterhouses and T-bones are steakhouse favorites. When cut 1½ inches (3.75cm) thick, the porterhouse is enough for at least two people and often served as a shareable plate. It comes from the rear end of the short loin, where both the strip steak and the tenderloin are larger and often more tender. The T-bone comes from the opposite side of the short loin, where the first few steaks have much smaller fillets. By law, a porterhouse fillet must be a minimum of 1¼ inches (3cm) wide to be considered a porterhouse. Anything less means it's an equally delicious T-bone. This recipe calls for a 1 ½-inch (3.75cm) thick porterhouse—Texas style, baby!

1½-inch (3.75cm) thick porterhouse

2 ½ tbsp ArnieTex Beef Seasoning Blend (page 25)

Wood chunks or chips (your preferred wood, but I like mesquite; optional)

1   Trim off any excess fat from around the steak. Rinse the steak and pat dry.

2   Moderately season the steak with ArnieTex Beef Seasoning Blend. Ensure that both sides and all edges are seasoned evenly.

3   Place the steak in an airtight container, and set in the refrigerator for at least 2 hours or up to 6 hours for maximum seasoning absorption. (In a pinch, 30 minutes is fine, which is about how long it will take to set your fire.) Remove the steaks from the refrigerator and allow them to sit out on the counter for 30 minutes before grilling.

4   Prepare the grill with one full charcoal chimney. Arrange the fire for direct grilling, and bring the cooking temperature to 450°F to 500°F (203°C to 260°C). Thoroughly clean the grates. For added smoke and flavor, add the wood chunks (if using) to the coals, ensuring they are emitting a thin blue or translucent smoke.

5   Lay the steak directly over the coals, and cook, flipping every 2 minutes to develop char. If the flames start to flare up, move the steak to an indirect cooking zone. Return the steak to the fire after it settles.

6   Check for doneness with a meat thermometer; the steaks should be at 135°F (57°C) in the thickest part for medium and to account for carry-over cooking during the rest time.

7   Transfer the steak to a serving plate or loosely wrap in foil and let rest for 5 to 7 minutes.

8   Serve, drizzled with all the natural au jus captured where it rested.

# STEAK
## [RIB EYE]

**PREP TIME**
7 minutes plus
2 hours to
marinate

**COOK TIME**
8 minutes

**SERVES**
2

The rib eye steak is my absolute favorite cut of meat to grill. Its tenderness and flavor are, to me, unmatched. Sure, it's perfectly fine to sear a rib eye in a frying pan or cast-iron skillet, basted with butter and rosemary, but when I'm on steak duty, you can bet that I'll be grilling these over mesquite coals for that extra-special flavor.

2 (1¼-inch/3cm thick) rib eye steaks

2½ tbsp ArnieTex Beef Seasoning Blend (page 25)

Wood chunks or chips (your preferred wood, but I like mesquite; optional)

1. Generously season the rib eyes with ArnieTex Beef Seasoning Blend. Ensure that both sides and all edges are seasoned evenly.

2. Place the steaks in an airtight container, and set in the refrigerator for at least 2 hours or up to 6 hours for maximum seasoning absorption. (In a pinch, 30 minutes is fine, which is about how long it will take to set your fire.) Remove the steaks from the refrigerator and allow them to sit out on the counter for 30 minutes before grilling.

3. Prepare the grill with one full charcoal chimney. Arrange the fire for direct grilling, and bring the cooking temperature to 450°F to 500°F (230°C to 260°C). Thoroughly clean the grates. For added smoke and flavor, add the wood chunks (if using) to the coals, ensuring they are emitting a thin blue or translucent smoke.

4. Lay the steaks directly over the coals, and cook, flipping every 2 minutes to develop char (char equals flavor). If the flames start to flare up, move the steaks to an indirect cooking zone. Return the steaks to the fire after it settles.

5. Check for doneness with a meat thermometer; the steaks should be at 135°F (57°C) in the thickest part for medium and to account for carry-over cooking during the rest time.

6. Transfer the steak to a serving plate or loosely wrap in foil and let rest for 5 to 7 minutes.

7. Serve, drizzled with all the natural au jus captured where it rested.

### PRO TIPS

*Ask your butcher or grocery store to cut you two rib eye steaks from the chuck end of the loin. The spinalis (the most tender part of the steak, also known as the "cap") is much larger on that end of the roast. For an extra tender bite, ask for a USDA Prime grade rib eye. USDA Choice grade is fine, but Prime is the most tender and flavorful.*

# CARNE GUISADA

**PREP TIME**
20 minutes

**COOK TIME**
1 hour 30 minutes

**SERVES**
8

When I was growing up, this dish was on the table at least once a week because my father loved it. (If he could have, he would have eaten beef three times a day.) This was one of his absolute favorites, to the point it was a common ingredient for breakfast tacos. Like many good things, Carne Guisada is a recipe that requires time and patience to make. If you commit to those two things, you will be rewarded with a velvety-smooth gravy and tender, melt-in-your-mouth meat. You'll see why this dish is such a staple in so many restaurants.

2 tbsp olive or vegetable oil

3 lb (1.35kg) chuck, cut into 1-inch (2.5cm) cubes

Water or beef or chicken broth, for deglazing

½ medium white onion, , coarsely chopped or sliced

3 garlic cloves, or 2 tsp granulated garlic

1 tsp whole black peppercorns, or ½ tsp black pepper

1¼ tsp cumin seeds, or 1 tsp ground cumin

2 tsp smoked paprika

½ stalk celery, finely diced

1 Roma tomato, diced

½ medium green bell pepper, ribs and seeds removed, and coarsely chopped or sliced

½ medium red bell pepper, ribs and seeds removed, and coarsely chopped or sliced

½ cup tomato sauce, or 2 tbsp tomato paste

1 tbsp salt

½ tsp dried Mexican oregano

1 bay leaf

3 tbsp all-purpose flour

1 Heat a 12-inch (30.cm) stainless-steel or cast-iron skillet over medium-high heat, and add the oil. When the oil is hot, add the chuck, in batches, and allow to brown for 3 to 5 minutes, stirring occasionally to ensure that all sides brown. (Don't crowd the meat in the pan, or you'll sacrifice browning due to moisture release.) Transfer the browned chuck to a plate, and repeat with the remaining meat.

2 If the fond (the caramelized bits) is stuck to the bottom of the skillet and looks like it will burn, you can add ¼ cup of water or broth to the pan to loosen it up. If you do, also add a little more oil to the pan for the next batch. (That fond is pure deliciousness, by the way.)

3 As you brown the last batch of meat, add the onion and cook until soft, about 8 minutes.

4 Grind the garlic cloves, whole black peppercorns, and cumin seeds using a molcajete (mortar and pestle). Transfer the ground garlic and spices, along with the paprika, to the middle of the skillet and allow to bloom. (If you're using granulated garlic and ground pepper and cumin, just add them all to the pan with the paprika.)

5 Return the browned chuck to the skillet. Pour in enough water to cover the meat by about a ½ inch (1.25cm). Add the celery, tomato, bell peppers, and tomato sauce, and stir to incorporate. Bring to a boil and then reduce the heat to low and simmer.

**6** Add the salt, oregano, and bay leaf, and stir. Cover and simmer for 1 hour, checking at the 30-minute mark to ensure the liquid is still covering the meat. If not, add additional hot water if needed.

**7** At the 45-minute mark, heat a 10-inch (25.5cm) skillet over medium heat, and add the flour. Stir the flour constantly until lightly golden, about 10 minutes. Do not burn the flour or it will be bitter. Reduce the heat if necessary, or pull the pan off the heat temporarily to control the browning.

**8** At the 1-hour mark, stir the 3 tablespoons of golden flour into a glass with ½ cup of cold water. Stir until the flour is fully incorporated with no clumps. Uncover the guiso and slowly pour in the entire mixture while stirring. After all the flour has been stirred in, cover the pan and simmer for 15 to 20 more minutes so the flour can thicken the gravy. Adjust with water if it's too thick; if it's too thin, remove the lid and simmer out some moisture to reach your desired consistency.

**9** When the beef is fork-tender, turn off the heat, remove the bay leaf, and allow to cool for 5 minutes. Serve with your favorite sides and warm flour tortillas.

### COOKING NOTES

*Every stove and pan are different, so this recipe may take longer on yours. I like to use a thick cast-iron skillet when making this. The best meat for this dish is a good ol' chuck. Chuck has so much collagen and fatty connective tissue that once it's all rendered, it makes the richest and most delectable gravy you've ever had. Sirloin is another popular cut. Some folks like to buy precut stew meat, but I prefer to cube mine into large, meaty chunks.*

*This guiso is great topped with Guacamole (page 208) or served alongside Pico de Gallo (page 34), a classic side salad made of thick-diced tomatoes and shredded iceberg lettuce, a fresh pot of pinto beans, and MommaTex's Mexican Rice (page 207), or the classic Tex-Mex twist of mashed potatoes (my favorite side with this dish). I like to eat it with flour tortillas to sop up any leftover gravy.*

# ASADO DE PUERCO

**PREP TIME**
20 minutes

**COOK TIME**
2 hours

**SERVES**
6

This pork stew recipe is known by many names. Asado de boda, puerco con chile colorado, or simply just "asado" are all commonly used when referencing this delicious dish. Some of these variations can be traced back to the Mexican states of Nuevo Leon and Zacatecas. Growing up in West Texas, my mom mostly called it asado, and when she told us it was ready, my siblings and I would run to the table.

2 tbsp pork lard or cooking oil, divided

2 lb (1kg) pork butt, cut into 1-inch (2.5cm) cubes

3 cups chicken broth

2 tsp salt

¼ tsp black pepper

1 tsp ground cumin

½ tsp dried Mexican oregano

**CHILE SAUCE**

5 chiles guajillo, deseeded, deveined, and rinsed well

2 chiles ancho, deseeded, deveined, and rinsed well

3 chiles de árbol, deseeded, deveined, and rinsed well (optional)

3 garlic cloves

1  To make the chile sauce, bring 4 cups of water to a boil In a 12-inch (30.5cm) saucepan placed over high heat. Once boiling, reduce the heat to medium, and bring the water to a simmer. Add the chiles guajillo, ancho, and de árbol (if using), and simmer for 10 minutes.

2  Add the garlic, turn off the heat, and let stand for 10 minutes to soften and cool.

3  Transfer the vegetables to a blender along with 1 cup of the cooking water, and blend to a fine puree. Strain through a sieve, and set aside.

4  Heat a 12-inch (30.5cm) skillet over medium-high heat, and add 1 tablespoon of lard. When the lard is hot, add half of the pork butt. (Be sure the meat isn't crowded in the pan.) Sear on all sides, about 6 to 8 minutes, and transfer to a plate.

5  Deglaze the pan with ¼ cup of water (regular or the chile cooking water), and pour the water and fond into a bowl. Set aside.

6  Add the remaining 1 tablespoon of lard to the skillet, and sear the rest of the pork. Transfer the rest of the pork to the plate.

7  Drain any excess oil from the pan. Deglaze the pan again with more water, and pour the water and fond into the bowl from step 5.

8  Return the pork to the pan, along with the chicken broth and the chile sauce. Ensure that the liquid covers the pork by at least ½ inch (1.25cm). Add the salt, pepper, cumin, and oregano, and stir well. Add the reserved water and fond, and stir well. Reduce the heat to medium, cover, and simmer until the meat is completely soft, up to 2 hours. Check at the 90-minute mark for tenderness.

9  Remove from the heat, and allow to rest for 5 minutes. Serve with corn or flour tortillas. It's also great with some Salsa Verde—Base (page 40) for a kick of heat.

# BOTANA
## [RGV STYLE]

**PREP TIME**
10 minutes

**COOK TIME**
5 minutes

**SERVES**
8

This recipe is not to be confused with the smaller appetizer found on menus in many American Tex-Mex restaurants. In South Texas, and particularly the Rio Grande Valley, botana is an extra large family-style platter with loads of components. This is more than a dish in our culture; it's a comfort-food meal served for many social occasions. In restaurants, it often can be ordered for between two and eight people, although it can always feed more people than advertised. Botana is served with tortillas so you can stuff tacos full with fajitas and the other ingredients. When people who have moved away from the Valley return, the first meal they want is a botana platter.

2 Roma tomatoes, diced

½ medium white onion, diced

½ cup sliced pickled jalapeños

Totopos (page 211)

Refried Beans—Three Ways, stage 1 (page 205)

12 oz (340g) American cheese, shredded

Fajitas—Restaurant Style (page 108)

Guacamole (page 208)

MommaTex's Mexican Rice (page 207)

1   Arrange the diced tomatoes, onion, and pickled jalapeños on three small plates. Set aside.

2   Preheat the broiler to 325°F (165°C).

3   Evenly arrange the Totopos on a baking sheet to cover the tray.

4   Cover the Totopos with the Refried Beans—Three Ways. The beans don't have to be even, but try to cover most of the chips, especially in the center of the tray.

5   Evenly sprinkle the cheese over the chips.

6   Place the baking sheet under the broiler until the cheese is melted, 3 to 5 minutes.

7   Remove from the oven. Top with the Fajitas—Restaurant Style, and serve immediately with the tomatoes, onion, jalapeños, Guacamole, and MommaTex's Mexican Rice on the side.

## COOKING NOTES

*Serve with fresh tortillas so you and your guests can make individual tacos to your preference.*

*Want to double up on the meat? It's also common to order a botana "mixta," with beef and chicken fajitas. Simply prepare the Chicken Fajitas (page 111) along with the Fajitas— Restaurant Style (page 108), and serve half of the botana with the beef and the other half with the chicken.*

# SOMBRERO PLATE

**PREP TIME**
20 minutes

**COOK TIME**
20 minutes

**SERVES**
4

While growing up in South Texas, one of my favorite dishes served in Mexican restaurants was the Sombrero Plate, probably so called because the crown of fresh corn tortillas that topped the dish resembled a little hat. The tortillas are perfectly placed to enable you to grab a whole taco full of meat and veggies and cheese with one hand, making this an ideal shareable plate. In certain regions of Mexico, Texas, and the Southwest, this is known as an alambre plate.

2 lb (1kg) fajitas (skirt steak)

2 tbsp canola oil

5 strips thick-cut bacon, diced

3 tsp salt

2 tsp black pepper

1 tsp garlic powder

1 medium white onion, sliced

1 medium green bell pepper, ribs and seeds removed, and sliced

1 Roma tomato, diced

1 bunch of fresh cilantro

15 oz (425g) grated Oaxaca cheese

6 medium corn tortillas

Jalapeño or serrano Chile Toreados (page 63) or Salsa Taquera (page 45)

1 Square up the skirt steak around the edges. Slice the meat in half, stack the two pieces, and cut in half again. Then, cutting across the grain, slice the meat into strips ¼ to ⅜ inch (0.5 to 1cm) thick. Cut the loose pieces of meat (left over from squaring it) into similar-sized strips. Place the strips in a large bowl.

2 Heat a griddle or large skillet over medium heat, and add the oil. Add the bacon, and cook until about halfway cooked, around 4 minutes.

3 Add the fajitas, and season with the salt, pepper, and garlic powder. Add the onion, cook for 3 minutes, and then add the bell pepper, tomato, and a few torn sprigs of cilantro. Turn off the heat, stir well to incorporate

4 Sprinkle the cheese over the top and then cover with a lid for 5 minutes so that the cheese can melt.

5 While the cheese is melting, warm the corn tortillas on a comal or in a skillet over medium heat for 1 or 2 minutes per side. Add the warm tortillas on top of the fajitas to form the "brim" of the hat. Add a final tortilla on center-top to give the dish a sombrero appearance.

6 Serve, grabbing a tortilla and pulling off lots of the filling goodness, with Chile Toreados or Salsa Taquera on the side.

## COOKING NOTES

*Oaxaca cheese is best in this recipe, but if you can't find it, you can substitute Monterey Jack or mozzarella instead. Be sure the corn tortillas are served warm so they're plenty pliable to be able to scoop up the filling.*

# STEAK RANCHERO

**PREP TIME**
15 minutes plus
30 minutes to
marinate

**COOK TIME**
20 minutes

**SERVES**
2

The word ranchero often appears on restaurant menus to designate that the dish comes with something sautéed and smothered in a delicious salsa roja, such as huevos rancheros or pork ranchero. This recipe is for my favorite ranchero plate—steak. Often it's served with sliced steak, but when I'm cooking, I serve the steaks whole. There's just something great about slicing off that first bite, as fresh as can be. Restaurants often serve thinner cuts of meat in this dish, but feel free to use your favorite cut of steak or fajita. I love to use sirloin or flap meat because of its tenderness. Your target thickness for the meat is about ½ to ¾ inch (1.25–2cm).

1½ lb (680g) flap meat

1½ tbsp ArnieTex Beef Seasoning Blend (page 25)

2 tbsp olive oil, divided

½ cup thinly sliced white onion

2 Roma tomatoes, sliced in half lengthwise and then across

1 garlic clove, minced

2 jalapeños, stems removed

2 tbsp chopped fresh cilantro leaves

1 Butterfly the flap meat, and square it up around the edges. Evenly season both sides of the steaks with the ArnieTex Beef Seasoning Blend. Place the meat in an airtight container, and set in the refrigerator for 30 minutes.

2 Heat a 12-inch (30.5cm) skillet over high heat, and add 1 tablespoon of oil. When the oil is hot, add the steaks and press down lightly with a spatula to ensure a good sear. Sear for 3 to 5 minutes, flip over, and sear the other side for 3 to 5 minutes. Check for doneness with a meat thermometer; the steaks should be at 135°F (57°C) for medium. Transfer the steaks to serving plates.

3 Add the remaining 1 tablespoon of oil to the skillet, immediately followed by the onion and tomatoes. Reduce the heat to medium, and sauté the vegetables, stirring constantly, for 3 minutes. Add the garlic, and sauté for 2 minutes. Add the jalapeños, and continue cooking, stirring, until all veggies are tender, 5 minutes. (The tomatoes will mostly fall apart. That's how you want them for the ranchero sauce.)

4 Turn off the heat, and liberally pour the ranchero sauce over the steaks. Garnish with cilantro, set 1 jalapeño next to each steak, and serve.

## COOKING NOTES

*I like to serve this with homemade french fries, rice, beans, and some warm flour tortillas. Although the steak is covered in salsa, I love to add a little Salsa Verde—Base (page 40), too.*

# TOSTADAS
## [AKA CHALUPAS]

It's an ongoing debate: Are tostadas the same as chalupas? I'm the first to agree that accuracy and history are important, and I've heard lots of arguments about the regionality and name differences between the two. Here in South Texas though, we're too busy chowing down on these tostadas and chalupas while using the names interchangeably. The best part about this recipe is that you can add any protein you want to make them uniquely your own.

★  ★

2 cups cooking oil

12 corn tortillas

3 cups Refried Beans—Three Ways, stage 3 (page 205)

1 cup shredded iceberg lettuce

4 Roma tomatoes, diced

1 medium white onion, diced

4 oz (115g) shredded cheddar or crumbled queso fresco

2 limes, cut into wedges

Your favorite salsa

1  Add the oil to a 12-inch (30.5cm) skillet, set over medium-high heat, and heat to 350°F (180°C). (This is for a shallow fry.)

2  Add each tortilla to the oil, one at a time, and fry for 2 minutes. Using tongs, flip the tortilla, and fry until golden brown on the other side, about 1 minute. If it needs more time, you can fry it for up to 30 seconds more. Using tongs, remove the tortilla from the oil, tilting it sideways to drain some of the excess oil, and transfer to a paper towel–lined plate. Repeat with the remaining tortillas.

3  Spread a thin layer of Refried Beans—Three Ways on each tortilla. Top with a layer of lettuce, followed by about 1 tablespoon each of tomatoes and onions per tortilla, and finish with some cheddar or queso fresco. Serve with lime wedges, and with your favorite salsa on the side.

## COOKING NOTES

*These tostadas or chalupas are fantastic as is, but you also could serve them topped with your favorite protein, Guacamole (page 208), sour cream, and Pico de Gallo (page 34).*

# CARNE CON PAPAS

I like to joke that I like "carne con papas … *not* papas con carne"—a lighthearted jab at some dishes that go easy on the beef. This is an easy recipe that's easily customizable with your preferred cut or preparation of beef, be it steak, fajitas, sirloin, chuck, or even ground beef. I prefer chuck because of the texture it brings to the finished dish. However, it does require a bit of a time commitment. For a quick version, use an 80/20 blend of ground beef. It is just as good and comforting.

★ ★ ★

2 tbsp cooking oil

1½ lb (680g) chuck, cut into 1-inch (2.5cm) cubes

½ medium white onion, diced medium

2 garlic cloves, minced

1½ tsp salt

2 dashes of black pepper

½ tsp ground cumin

⅓ medium green bell pepper, ribs and seeds removed, and diced medium

1 Roma tomato, diced medium

2 tbsp tomato sauce

3 cups chicken broth, warmed

1 bay leaf

2 medium russet potatoes, cut into 1-inch (2.5cm) cubes

1 Heat a 12-inch (30.5cm) stainless-steel or cast-iron skillet over medium-high heat, and add the oil. When the oil is hot, add the chuck, in batches, and begin to brown on all sides, about 3 to 5 minutes per batch. (Don't crowd the meat in the pan, or you'll sacrifice browning due to moisture release.) Transfer the browned chuck to a plate, and repeat with the remaining meat.

2 During the last batch, reduce the heat to medium. Add the onions, and cook, stirring, for 2 minutes.

3 Add the garlic, salt, pepper, cumin, bell pepper, and tomato, and cook, stirring frequently, for 2 minutes. Return the browned chuck to the skillet.

4 Add the tomato sauce and warm chicken broth. The meat should be fully covered by the broth, but you can add water to fully cover if needed.

5 When it starts to simmer, stir to loosen the fond (the caramelized bits) on the bottom of the pan. Reduce the heat to low, add the bay leaf, cover, and continue to cook for 1½ hours.

6 Add the potatoes, and cook until the potatoes are fork-tender, 20 to 30 minutes.

7 Remove the bay leaf. Taste and adjust the salt if needed (especially if you added water in step 4), and serve.

## PRO TIPS

*This is delicious served with some queso fresco and warm tortillas. Also some Salsa Verde—Tomatillos (page 42) will amp up the heat if desired.*

PREP TIME
20 minutes

COOK TIME
1½ hours

SERVES
6 to 8

# CALDO DE POLLO

Caldo de Pollo is said to have magical powers—it can heal the sick and cure the soul of sadness. This recipe is an underrated Mexican superfood, packed with protein from the chicken and a hearty broth full of vitamins and nutrients. In our culture, whenever a kid gets sick, Mama gets the Caldo de Pollo going! It's the epitome of a comfort food—so much so that there's a running joke that endearingly pokes fun at our matriarchs who prepare this recipe even in the hottest of weather. This recipe is that great.

- 4–5lb (1.75–2.25kg) whole chicken, cut in primal cuts, rinsed well
- 2 ears of corn, cut in 2-inch (5cm) sections (6 or 7 sections)
- 2 carrots, cut into ¾ to 1 inch (2–2.5cm) slices
- 2 celery stalks, cut into 2-inch (5cm) pieces
- 1 jalapeño, stem removed
- 1 medium white onion, quartered
- 4 garlic cloves, smashed
- 1 tbsp salt
- ¼ tsp black pepper
- 2 tsp ground cumin
- 2 large russet potatoes, quartered
- 1 calabaza squash, cut into ¾- to 1-inch (2–2.5cm) slices
- ½ cup chopped fresh cilantro
- MommaTex's Mexican Rice (page 207)
- 2 limes, quartered

1 Add the chicken to a 10-quart (9.5-liter) stockpot, and fill the pot with water to cover the chicken by 4 inches (10cm). Set over medium-high heat, and bring to a boil. Reduce the heat to medium, cover, and cook for 45 minutes.

2 Uncover and add the corn, carrots, celery, jalapeño, onion, and garlic to the chicken. Season with salt, pepper, and cumin. Stir, bring back to a slow simmer, then cover and cook for 15 minutes.

3 Add the potatoes and calabaza, and cook for 15 more minutes.

4 Taste the broth for salt and adjust with ¼ teaspoon salt at a time if needed, stirring between additions.

5 If the potatoes are fork-tender at this point, the caldo is done. If not, continue cooking in 10-minute increments until the potatoes are fork-tender. Turn off the heat.

6 Stir in the cilantro, and allow the caldo to set for 10 minutes.

7 Serve with MommaTex's Mexican Rice and a quartered lime on the side to squeeze into the bowl.

# ARROZ CON POLLO

**PREP TIME**
15 minutes

**COOK TIME**
25 minutes

**SERVES**
3

Arroz con Pollo is undeniably a top comfort food any time of year. Restaurants use a lot of different techniques for this recipe—some are slightly soupy with a bit of extra broth to slurp up along with every bite, and some have very little liquid at all, if any, making for a more texture-filled bite. I like to make mine somewhere in between, so that's what you'll find with this warm and hearty recipe.

2 tbsp cooking oil, divided

3 deboned chicken thighs, cut into 1½-inch (3.75cm) strips

⅓ medium white onion, sliced

¾ cup white rice

½ tsp salt

1 dash of black pepper

½ tsp ground cumin

¼ tsp dried Mexican oregano

2 cups low-sodium chicken broth

¼ cup tomato sauce

1  Heat a 10-inch (25.5cm) skillet over medium-high heat, and add 1 tablespoon of the oil. Add the chicken, and begin to sear, stirring, for 3 to 5 minutes.

2  Add the onions and sauté for another 2 minutes. Remove the pan from the heat, and set aside on the stove.

3  In a second 10-inch (25.5cm) skillet over medium heat, add the remaining 1 tablespoon of oil. When the oil is hot, add the rice and stir frequently as it begins to brown, 3 minutes.

4  Add the salt, pepper, cumin, and oregano, and stir quickly for 15 seconds.

5  Add the chicken broth and tomato sauce, and stir to incorporate.

6  Add the chicken and juices from the first pan and stir. Reduce the heat to medium-low, bring to a low simmer, and cook for 15 minutes.

7  Turn off the heat. Let the pan rest for 5 minutes, and serve.

# CALABAZA CON POLLO

This dish is a South Texas favorite, where it is served in homes, restaurants, and even behind the counter of convenience stores. The hot broth with bites of crunchy calabaza and tender chicken make this both a superfood and a comfort food. Calabaza is also commonly known as a summer squash, or a Mexican zucchini; at grocery stores, it often is called a calabacita. Calabaza is slightly more dense in texture than a zucchini with a hint of sweetness.

4 tbsp cooking oil, divided

2 ears of corn, shucked and cut off the cob, or 6 oz (170g) canned corn, drained

¼ medium white onion, diced

3 medium calabazas, cut into 1-inch (2.5cm) cubes

1 Roma tomato, diced

1½ lb (680g) boneless skinless chicken thighs, cut into 1½-inch (3.75cm) pieces

½ tsp ground cumin

1 tsp granulated garlic

¼ tsp black pepper

¼ cup tomato sauce

4 cups chicken broth

1  Heat a 12-inch (30.5cm) skillet over medium heat, and add 2 tablespoons of the oil. When the oil is hot, add the corn and sauté for 2 minutes.

2  Add the onions, and sauté for 2 minutes.

3  Add the calabaza and tomatoes, and sauté for 2 minutes. Transfer the cooked vegetables to a bowl.

4  Add the remaining 2 tablespoons of oil to the pan, and increase the heat to medium-high. Add the chicken, and sauté for 4 or 5 minutes. The chicken will begin to turn a golden-brown color and leave a little fond (the caramelized bits) on the bottom of the pan.

5  Add the cumin, garlic, and pepper, and sauté, stirring constantly to incorporate, for 1 minute.

6  Return the cooked vegetables to the pan, add the tomato sauce, and pour in the chicken broth. It should slightly cover all the ingredients in the pan. Bring to a simmer, stirring to scrape the fond off the bottom of the pan. Reduce the heat to medium, cover, and simmer for 15 minutes. If it's boiling too fast, reduce the heat a bit more.

7  Serve in a bowl with warm corn tortillas. No other sides needed; this is a complete, filling, and delicious meal in one bowl.

## COOKING NOTES

*To amp up the heat, you can add 1 or 2 teaspoons of Salsa Verde—Base (page 40) on top of the individual bowls as you serve it.*

# CHILE COLORADO

**PREP TIME**
20 minutes

**COOK TIME**
2 hours, 10 minutes

**SERVES**
5

In Mexico, chile colorado simply means "red" or "colored red." So it's an appropriate name for this recipe, which is made of tender chunks of beef that are smothered in a bright red chile sauce. This recipe began to take root in the late 1800s to mid 1900s, when the San Antonio Chili Queens began cooking for the San Antonio community during one of its boom eras of development. Like many regional recipes, the ingredients can vary widely, and this is my family's take on the classic.

★ ★ ★

2 lb (1kg) chuck
4 tbsp cooking oil, divided
2 cups chicken or beef broth
½ medium white onion, diced
4 garlic cloves, minced
1 bay leaf

**CHILE COLORADO SAUCE**
18 chiles guajillo, deseeded and rinsed
8 garlic cloves
1 medium white onion, quartered
2 Roma tomatoes

2 tsp tomato paste
1 tsp dried Mexican oregano
1 tsp cumin
2 tsp salt, plus more as needed
½ tsp black pepper

1  To make the chile colorado sauce, add the chiles guajillo, garlic cloves, and onion to a stockpot. Fill with just enough water to cover the ingredients, set over medium-high heat, and bring to a boil. Reduce the heat to low, and simmer for 10 minutes.

2  Turn off the heat and allow to sit for 5 minutes to continue to soften.

3  Transfer the cooked ingredients to a blender. Reserve 2 cups of the cooking water.

4  Add the reserved cooking water, tomatoes, tomato paste, oregano, cumin, salt, and pepper to the blender, and blend on high until smooth.

5  Using a sieve, pour the liquid out of the blender and strain out any chili flakes. Use the back of a spoon to press the liquid from the chile flakes until you have expressed all the liquid. Set aside the sauce.

6  Cut the chuck into approximately 1-inch (2.5cm) cubes. Discard any big, hard fat pieces.

7  Heat a heavy-bottomed 12-inch (30.5cm) skillet over medium-high heat, and add 2 tablespoons of oil. When the oil is hot, add half of the chuck and sear all sides, stirring occasionally, for 5 to 8 minutes. Be careful not to crowd the skillet, or the meat won't sear as well. Transfer the seared meat to a bowl.

8  Add ½ cup of broth or water to the skillet to loosen the fond, and pour it over the beef in the bowl.

9  Reheat the skillet over high heat. Add the remaining 2 tablespoons of oil, and sear the remaining meat on all sides, stirring occasionally, for 5 to 8 minutes.

10  Return the first batch of meat to the skillet.

11  Add the diced onion, reduce the heat to medium, and sauté for 4 minutes. Add the minced garlic, and sauté for 1 minute. Add 4 cups of chile colorado sauce and enough broth to cover the meat by at least ½ to ¾ inch (1.25cm to 2cm). Add the bay leaf. Cover and cook at a low simmer, stirring occasionally, for 1½ hours.

12  At the 1-hour mark, taste for seasoning and add salt if needed. Cover again, and cook for 30 minutes. Check for tenderness. If not fully tender, cook for 30 more minutes. Serve with fresh tortillas.

## COOKING NOTES

*You'll have an extra 1 cup of the chile colorado sauce. Store the leftover sauce in an airtight container in the refrigerator for up to 2 weeks or in the freezer for up to 3 months, and use in your preferred recipe.*

# FLAUTAS

**PREP TIME**
15 minutes

**COOK TIME**
35 minutes

**SERVES**
5

Flautas can be prepared, filled, and garnished in endless ways. My mom boiled the chicken and then finely shredded it for her flautas. This is a slightly modified version of her recipe; I sauté the ingredients before chopping and stuffing. Although similar to taquitos, flautas usually use larger corn tortillas so there's also more fillings.

★ ★ ★

1 tbsp cooking oil

1 lb (450g) boneless, skinless chicken thighs, cut across into ½-inch (1.25cm) strips

3 garlic cloves, diced

1 Roma tomato, diced

¼ medium white onion, diced

½ cup chicken broth

1 tsp salt

1 dash of black pepper

2 cups frying oil, divided

15 corn tortillas

15 toothpicks

⅓ cup Mexican crema

**SALAD**

½ head of iceberg lettuce, shredded

1 Roma tomato, diced

1 tbsp roughly chopped cilantro leaves

1 cup crumbled queso fresco

1  To make the salad, combine the lettuce, tomato, cilantro, and queso fresco in a large bowl. Cover with plastic wrap, and set in the refrigerator while you prepare the flautas.

2  Heat a 10-inch (25.5cm) skillet over high heat, and add the cooking oil. When the oil is hot, add the chicken and sauté for 5 minutes. Add the onion, and sauté for 1 minute. Add the tomato and garlic, and sauté for 1 minute.

3  Add the chicken broth, salt, and pepper, and bring to a simmer. Stir to loosen the fond at the bottom of the skillet, cover, and simmer for 5 minutes. Uncover, stir, and simmer uncovered for 5 more minutes to evaporate some of the liquid.

4  Transfer the ingredients to a bowl to cool for 2 to 3 minutes, then transfer to a cutting board and finely chop all the ingredients together. Return to the bowl.

5  Clean the skillet, and set over medium-high heat. Add 1 cup of frying oil and bring to a light simmer. Quickly lay each tortilla into the oil, flip once, and immediately remove to a plate. This should take no more than 10 seconds. Stack the oiled tortillas on a plate.

6  Add the remaining 1 cup of frying oil to the skillet, and heat the oil while you assemble the flautas. To assemble the flautas, add 1 heaping tablespoon of chicken to each tortilla, spread it out into an even layer, and roll up the tortilla snugly. Use one or two toothpicks to seal the tortillas.

7  Increase the skillet heat to medium-high, about 310°F to 325°F (155°C to 165°C). Add up to 4 flautas at a time in the shallow oil, and fry, using tongs to roll over each flauta, until they're an even, golden-brown color, 1 or 2 minutes per side.

8  Transfer the flautas to a cooling rack set on a baking sheet to drain, and repeat with the remaining flautas. Once cool, remove the toothpicks.

9  Serve 3 flautas per plate, topped with 1 cup of salad, 1 tablespoon of Mexican crema, and some queso fresco, with your favorite salsa on the side.

# PICADILLO

**PREP TIME**
5 minutes

**COOK TIME**
20 minutes

**SERVES**
6

Picadillo is a popular dish in Mexico, Cuba, and the Philippines, and each region has its own unique interpretation. This South Texas version is quite a bit different from even the Mexican version. Picadillo is one of those dishes in which at least a couple frozen vegetables are not only okay to use, but also expected for that homemade feel. Picadillo goes well with a side of MommaTex's Mexican Rice (page 207) and Basic Beans—Traditional (page 204) with tortillas on the side.

★ ★ ★

1 tbsp cooking oil
2 lb (1kg) 80/20 ground beef
½ medium white onion, diced
2 garlic cloves, minced
½ tsp ground cumin
1½ tsp salt
½ tsp black pepper

2 cups chicken broth or water
2 Roma tomatoes, diced
¼ cup tomato sauce
1 large russet potato, small diced
2 small carrots, small diced
¼ cup frozen green peas

¼ cup frozen corn kernels
¼ tsp dried Mexican oregano
½ medium green bell pepper, ribs and seeds removed, and diced
2 jalapeños
¼ cup chopped fresh cilantro

1   Heat a large skillet over high heat, and add the oil. When the oil is hot, add the ground beef and char for 20 to 30 seconds. Using a wooden spoon, break up the meat a bit, and continue to char until the meat is about halfway browned, about 4 to 6 minutes.

2   Add the onions, stir, and cook for 2 minutes.

3   Add the garlic, cumin, salt, and pepper, and cook, stirring frequently, for 1 minute.

4   Pour in the chicken broth. It should cover the meat completely. Add the tomatoes, tomato sauce, potatoes, carrots, peas, corn, oregano, bell pepper, and the whole jalapeños. Reduce the heat to medium, cover, and simmer for 10 minutes.

5   Add the cilantro, and stir to incorporate. The beef will be fully cooked at this point, but check the potatoes with a fork to see if they are fully cooked. If not, cover and simmer for up to 5 more minutes.

6   Turn off the heat, and let the pan rest, covered, for 5 minutes before serving.

# ENCHILADAS ROJAS

**PREP TIME**
15 minutes

**COOK TIME**
20 minutes

**SERVES**
5

Corn and chiles are two of the defining ingredients of pre-Colombian cuisine, and this Enchiladas Rojas recipe has roots that go back that far. Have fun with this dish, modifying the type and amount of chile sauces as you like, and try stuffing the tortillas with different vegetables or proteins. (Beef or chicken work well.) This is a historic dish that has evolved to please so many palates.

★ ★ ★

1 cup cooking oil

15 corn tortillas

2 cups Chile Guajillo Sauce (page 56), warmed

15 oz (425g) queso fresco, crumbled, plus more for topping

½ head iceberg lettuce, shredded

1 medium white onion, sliced

2 Roma tomatoes, diced

1 lime, cut into wedges

1  Preheat the oven to 350°F (180°C).

2  Heat a 10-inch (25.5cm) skillet over medium heat, and add the oil. When the oil is hot, use tongs to dip each tortilla in the oil for 5 to 10 seconds per side—just enough to coat in the oil and make the tortillas rollable. Tilt the tortillas to allow the excess oil to drain back into the pan. Stack the dipped tortillas on a plate, and repeat with the remaining tortillas.

3  Now dip each tortilla in the Chile Guajillo Sauce to completely coat. Lay each dipped tortilla on a baking sheet, and repeat with the remaining tortillas.

4  Add a line of queso fresco to each tortilla, about 2 tablespoons, and then fold one edge of the tortilla over the cheese and continue rolling until the tortilla encloses the cheese. Place the rolled tortilla seam side down on a baking sheet, and repeat with the remaining queso fresco and tortillas, setting them side by side on the baking sheet.

5  Bake for 15 minutes.

6  Remove the baking sheet from the oven, pour the remaining warm Chile Guajillo Sauce over the enchiladas, and top with more crumbled queso fresco to your preference.

7  Evenly divide the enchiladas among 5 plates (3 per plate). Serve with lettuce, onion, and tomatoes on the side, along with a slice of lime.

## PRO TIPS

*These enchiladas are great topped with avocado slices and Salsa Roja—Boiled (page 38). They're also good served alongside rice and beans.*

# ENCHILADAS SUIZAS

**PREP TIME**
15 minutes

**COOK TIME**
20 minutes

**SERVES**
5

Suizas are one of the most popular variations of enchiladas. This recipe wasn't a staple in my family when I was growing up, but it only took one bite for me to become hooked on them. These enchiladas get their name from the dairy component of the dish—Suizas means "Swiss"— which perfectly complements the deliciously tart salsa verde they're smothered in.

★ ★ ★

1 lb (450g) boneless, skinless chicken breast

1 tsp ArnieTex Poultry Seasoning Blend (page 25)

2 garlic cloves

¼ medium white onion

1 cup frying oil

12 corn tortillas

12 oz (340g) shredded queso Oaxaca, queso Chihuahua, or Monterey Jack cheese

1 bunch of chopped fresh cilantro

1 cup diced white onion

1 cup Mexican crema

**SALSA VERDE**

2 jalapeños

½ cup diced white onion

9 tomatillos, husks removed

3 garlic cloves

1 poblano

1 cup chopped fresh cilantro

4 oz (115g) cream cheese

¼ cup Mexican crema

½ tsp salt

2 tsp chicken bouillon

1 tbsp cooking oil

1   Add the chicken breast, ArnieTex Chicken Seasoning Blend, garlic, and onion to a 4-quart (4-liter) saucepan. Pour in enough water to fully cover the ingredients by 2 inches (5cm), and set over medium heat. Bring to a low boil and cook for 15 minutes. Turn off the heat, and allow the ingredients to cool in the water for 10 minutes. Transfer the chicken and vegetables to a bowl. Reserve ½ cup of the chicken-stock water.

2   To make the salsa verde, fill an 8-quart (7.5-liter) stockpot half full of water, and set over medium-high heat. Add the jalapeños and diced onion, and bring to a slow boil. Add the tomatillos and garlic, and cook until the tomatillos become slightly opaque, up to 8 minutes. When all the vegetables are softened, no more than 10 minutes, transfer them to a bowl.

3   Roast the poblano over a stove flame or on a comal or griddle, turning often to char all sides. Wrap the poblano tightly in foil, and set aside for 15 minutes. Remove the poblano from the foil, peel off the skin, and remove the seeds and ribs from the inside.

4   Add the cooked chiles, diced onion, tomatillos, and 3 garlic cloves to a blender. Add the cilantro, cream cheese, Mexican crema, salt, and chicken bouillon, along with ¼ cup of reserved chicken-stock water, and blend to a creamy, loose consistency, adding 1 tablespoon more chicken-stock water at a time if needed.

5   Heat a 12-inch (30.5cm) skillet or saucepan over medium heat, and add 1 tablespoon cooking oil. When the oil is hot, add the salsa verde, and cook, stirring often, for 10 minutes. Remove from the heat, and transfer to a large, shallow bowl to cool.

6   When the chicken is cool, shred it with forks or by using a hand mixer. Add ½ cup of the salsa verde to the chicken, and mix well.

7   Preheat the oven to 350°F (180°C).

8   Heat a 10-inch (25.5cm) skillet over medium-high heat, add 1 cup frying oil, and bring to a light simmer. Quickly lay each tortilla into the oil, flip it once, and immediately remove to a plate. This should take no more than 10 seconds per side. Stack the oiled tortillas on a separate plate.

9   Spread half of the salsa verde in an even layer in the bottom of a 9 × 13-inch (23 × 33cm) baking pan.

10  Coat each tortilla in the remaining salsa verde in the bowl. Add 1 to 2 heaping tablespoons of the chicken mixture to each coated tortilla, spread it out into an even layer, and roll up the tortilla snugly. Place the filled tortillas seam side down next to each other in the baking pan so they hold their shape. Cover the tops of the tortillas with a generous amount of the remaining salsa verde, and evenly sprinkle the cheese over the top.

11  Bake for 10 to 15 minutes or until the cheese is evenly melted.

12  Remove from the oven, and allow to cool for 5 minutes. Serve 3 enchiladas per plate, topped with cilantro, diced onions, and a drizzle of Mexican crema.

### PRO TIPS

*Using an electric hand mixer to shred cooked chicken is a poorly kept secret but an absolute game-changer to speed up the shredding process. Simply place the chicken in a mixing bowl and use a hand mixer on low to medium to shred it in about a minute.*

# TEXAS CHILI ENCHILADAS

This fun and delicious take on enchiladas has been in my family for three generations. This recipe is an incredibly easy version of the classic Mexican dish, yet the name is perhaps a bit tongue-in-cheek because there probably isn't very much chile guajillo, or any chile, in a canned chili. Nonetheless, that's part of what makes this dish so iconic and truly a Tex-Mex staple in origin and popularity.

★ ★ ★

1 cup cooking oil

12 corn tortillas

3 cups shredded cheddar

15-oz (425g) can chili (no beans), warmed

½ medium white onion, diced

1   Preheat the oven to 300°F (150°C).

2   In a 10-inch (25.5cm) skillet over medium-high heat, add the oil. When the oil is hot, use tongs to dip each tortilla in the oil for 5 to 10 seconds per side—just to make the tortillas rollable. Tilt the tortillas to allow the excess oil to drain back into the pan. Stack the dipped tortillas on a plate, and repeat with the remaining tortillas.

3   Lay the dipped tortillas in a single layer on a baking sheet. Add a large pinch of cheddar in a line on each tortilla and then fold one edge of the tortilla over the cheese and continue rolling until the tortilla encloses the cheese. Place the rolled tortilla seam side down on a baking sheet, and repeat with the remaining cheddar and tortillas, setting them side by side on the baking sheet.

4   Evenly pour the warmed chili over the tortillas and then top with the remaining cheese. Loosely cover with foil.

5   Bake for 15 minutes.

6   Remove from the oven and allow to cool for 10 minutes. Serve 3 enchiladas per plate, topped with diced onion, and with your favorite sides.

## PRO TIPS

*The choice of toppings for these enchiladas is up to you. Some like to top them with Mexican crema, avocado, Pico de Gallo (page 34), or no topping at all. I love to stack a classic side salad (shredded iceberg lettuce, diced tomatoes, sliced white onions, and a squeeze of lime) on top and cover the salad with whatever salsa is on the table. This to me, is one of the best bites from my childhood.*

# TEX-MEX ENCHILADAS

**PREP TIME**
10 minutes

**COOK TIME**
25 minutes

**SERVES**
5

Enchiladas are an iconic dish in Tex-Mex cuisine, where they have come into their own, combining traditional ingredients and bold flavors from Mexican cuisine with a distinctly American twist. Every home, restaurant, and region has its own variation of these enchiladas. The rich chili sauce and the smothering of American cheese here exemplify the cross-cultural nature of this dish.

★ ★ ★

1 tbsp plus 1 cup cooking oil, divided

1 lb (450g) 80/20 ground beef

15 corn tortillas

10 oz (285g) grated American or cheddar cheese

**ENCHILADA SAUCE**

3 tbsp all-purpose flour

2 tsp granulated garlic

1 tsp granulated onion

1½ tsp ground cumin

⅛ tsp black pepper

1 tbsp cooking oil

2½ cups unsalted chicken broth or water, divided

2 tbsp light chili powder

1 tbsp smoked paprika

2 tsp chicken bouillon

1 tbsp tomato paste

2 tsp salted butter

½ tsp salt

1  Preheat the oven to 350°F (180°C).

2  Heat a 10-inch (25.5cm) skillet over medium-high heat, and add 1 tablespoon of oil. When the oil is hot, add the ground beef and cook, breaking it up and stirring often, until it is done, about 6 minutes. Remove from the heat and set aside. (You do not need to drain the oil.)

3  Make the enchilada sauce: Heat another 10-inch (25.5cm) skillet over medium heat. Add the flour, and cook, stirring constantly, until golden, about 3 minutes.

4  Form a well in the middle of the flour, and add the granulated garlic, granulated onion, cumin, and pepper. Stir for 30 seconds. Form another well in the flour mixture, add 1 tablespoon of oil, and stir constantly until it all comes together.

5  Slowly add ½ cup of broth, and stir to incorporate. Add the chili powder, paprika, and bouillon, and stir for 20 to 30 seconds. Slowly whisk in the remaining 2 cups of broth, about ½ cup at a time, to form the sauce.

6  Add the tomato paste, butter, and salt, and continue to whisk until the sauce is smooth. Reduce the heat to medium-low, and simmer for 10 minutes while continuing to whisk every 30 seconds to 1 minute to prevent sticking.

7  Heat a third 10-inch (25.5cm) skillet over medium heat, and add the remaining 1 cup of oil. When the oil is hot, use tongs to dip each tortilla in the oil for 5 to 10 seconds per side—just enough to coat in the oil and make the tortillas rollable. Tilt the tortillas to allow the excess oil to drain back into the pan. Stack the dipped tortillas on a plate, and repeat with the remaining tortillas.

8  Set the skillet of ground beef over medium-low heat. Add ¼ cup of the enchilada sauce to the skillet, and stir to incorporate and reheat the beef.

9  Add a thin layer of the enchilada sauce to the bottom of a 9 × 12-inch (23 × 30.5cm) baking dish, about ¼ cup.

10  Fill each tortilla with 2 tablespoons of ground beef and a sprinkle of cheese. Roll the tortilla carefully, and place it seam side down in the baking dish. Repeat with the remaining beef and tortillas.

11  Pour the rest of the sauce evenly over the enchiladas. Sprinkle the remaining cheese over the top. Cover the pan with foil. Bake for 15 minutes.

12  Serve 3 enchiladas per plate. These are great alongside MommaTex's Mexican Rice (page 207), Charro Beans (page 202), and a side salad of shredded iceberg lettuce and diced tomatoes.

## COOKING NOTES

*Tex-Mex cuisine is known for its willingness to incorporate yellow (American) cheese into traditional recipes like this one. If the amount of cheese called for in this recipe isn't enough for your preference, I encourage you to use as much as you like. Don't forget to take a picture of that cheese pull! And for an added element of flavor and finish, instead of baking, you can broil the enchiladas at 400°F (200°C) for 3 to 7 minutes. If your oven has only one temperature setting, be sure the cheese doesn't burn.*

## PRO TIPS

*For a bit of a kick, add a dollop of Salsa Verde—Base (page 40) on top of the individual bowls as you serve them. The boiled chiles along with the garlic in the salsa will boost the flavor (and the heat) of this dish several notches.*

# CALDO DE RES

**PREP TIME**
15 minutes

**COOK TIME**
2½ hours

**SERVES**
6 to 8

Caldo de Res is my favorite soup. The cook time is a bit longer to coax out the bone marrow, break down the connective tissue, render the fat, and infuse the broth with all the delicious beefy flavor, but you'll be rewarded for your patience! I've made this recipe with beef ribs, oxtails, short ribs, and even brisket, all of which are perfectly delicious and acceptable. However, after many tests, I came to the conclusion that my abuela Leandra was right all along—beef shank is the best!

½ lb (225g) beef soup bones

2 lb (1kg) beef shank (usually sold in four 1-inch/2.5cm thick-cut shanks)

2 tbsp salt, plus more to taste

1 tsp black pepper

2 tsp ground cumin

1 medium white onion, quartered

2 celery stalks, cut into ½-inch (1.25cm) slices

5 garlic cloves, smashed

2 ears of corn, cut in 2-inch (5cm) sections (6 or 7 sections)

2 medium carrots, peeled and cut into ½-inch (1.25cm) slices

¼ cup tomato sauce

2 Roma tomatoes

⅓ head of green cabbage

2 medium russet potatoes, peeled and quartered

2 medium calabaza squash, cut into ¾- to 1-inch (2–2.5cm) slices

2 medium zucchinis, cut into ¾- to 1-inch (2 to 2.5cm) slices

½ cup chopped fresh cilantro

MommaTex's Mexican Rice (page 207)

2 limes, quartered

1  Add the soup bones to a 10-quart (9.5-liter) stockpot with 1 gallon (3.8 liters) of water. Set over medium-high heat, and bring to a boil. Reduce the heat to medium-low, and simmer for 30 minutes.

2  As the beef bones begin to cook, skim off the froth that floats to the top of the broth. After 30 minutes, add the shanks, salt, pepper, and cumin. Simmer for 1 hour, continuing to skim the froth from the top of the broth as needed.

3  While the broth simmers, be sure to keep it a minimum of 4 inches (10cm) above the meat. Add more water as needed.

4  After 1 hour, add the onion, celery, garlic, corn, carrots, tomato sauce, and tomatoes. Stir, and simmer for 30 more minutes.

5  Add the cabbage, potatoes, calabaza, and zucchini, stir, and simmer for 20 more minutes.

6  Taste the broth for salt and adjust with ¼ teaspoon at a time if needed, stirring thoroughly between additions.

7  If the potatoes are fork-tender at this point, the caldo is done. If not, stir and continue to cook in 10-minute increments until the potatoes are fork-tender. Turn off the heat.

8  Stir in the cilantro, and allow the caldo to set for 10 minutes.

9  Serve with MommaTex's Mexican Rice and with a quartered lime on the side to squeeze into the bowl.

# CEVICHE

**PREP TIME**
35 minutes plus
3 hours to
marinate

**COOK TIME**
none

**MAKES**
6 cups

Ceviche is a perfectly balanced appetizer or light entrée that packs a natural sweetness from the fish that's complemented by salt, acid, and a little bit of heat. This recipe is "cooked" by curing the seafood in lime or lemon juice. This is a simple version that leans on the familiar flavor of pico de gallo to create a South Texas staple. It's best served chilled with Totopos (page 211) or Tostadas (aka Chalupas) (page 133) with a base of Guacamole (page 208).

Juice of 7 to 9 limes (1 cup juice)

Juice of 5 to 7 lemons (1 cup juice)

½ lb (225g) fresh jumbo gulf shrimp

1 lb (450g) fresh halibut or red snapper, cut into ½-inch (1.25cm) cubes

½ tsp salt

⅛ tsp black pepper

3 cups cold Pico de Gallo (page 34)

1 avocado

1  Squeeze the limes and lemons into a glass container. Cover and set in the refrigerator.

2  Rinse the shrimp thoroughly, remove the outer skin, and devein. Rinse once more. Cut the shrimp into ½-inch (1.25cm) pieces.

3  Place the shrimp and fish in a large glass or stainless-steel bowl. Add the lemon juice, lime juice, salt, and pepper, and stir thoroughly to ensure that the fish and shrimp are completely submerged in the juices and seasonings.

4  Cover the bowl and refrigerate for at least 3 hours. The fish and shrimp will turn opaque and firm during this time, becoming fully "cooked."

5  When the fish and shrimp are cooked, drain most of the juice, reserving just a little in the bowl.

6  Add the Pico de Gallo to the fish and shrimp, and toss well.

7  Peel, pit, and seed the avocado, and cut it into cubes. (Don't do this ahead of time, or the avocado will turn brown.) Add the avocado on top of the ceviche, and serve immediately.

## COOKING NOTES

*When making the Pico de Gallo for this ceviche, reduce the salt to ½ teaspoon to account for the salt used in the cured fish and shrimp.*

# POLLO GUISADO

This delicious recipe is another childhood favorite from my mother's hand. The juicy, tender chicken stew comes together quickly and easily and the vegetables and seasonings make a heartwarming eating experience, especially with a corn tortilla.

2 tbsp olive oil

1 lb (450g) boneless, skinless chicken thighs, cut across to about ⅜ to ½ inch (1cm–1.25cm) thick

⅓ medium white onion, julienned

2 garlic cloves, minced

1 scallion, julienned

1 tbsp green bell pepper, julienned

1 medium Roma tomato, julienned

1 cup salted chicken broth

½ tsp salt

1 dash of black pepper

½ tsp ground cumin

2 tsp tomato paste, or ¼ cup tomato sauce

1 Heat a 12-inch (30.5cm) heavy-bottomed saucepan or skillet over medium-high heat, and add the oil. When the oil is hot, add the chicken and sauté, stirring and turning over the meat to brown all sides evenly, for 5 minutes.

2 Reduce the heat to medium. Add the onions, and sauté for 2 minutes.

3 Add the garlic, scallion, bell peppers, and tomato, and sauté for 1 minute.

4 Pour in the chicken broth, and add the salt, pepper, cumin, and tomato paste. Stir to incorporate, cover, and simmer for 10 minutes.

5 After 10 minutes, taste and adjust the salt if needed.

6 Remove from the heat and allow to set for 5 minutes before serving.

**7**

# MI RANCHITO

## PRO TIPS

It's traditional to serve oneself directly from the disco and to make just about as many tacos as you can handle (or as are socially acceptable!) No sides needed; just enjoy the amazing flavors that have melded together to become a single, delicious taco filling. An added bonus of the disco is that you can warm your tortillas directly on it: dip them in a bit of the juice in the pan, and heat them on the upper edge of the disco.

# DISCADA NORTEÑA

**PREP TIME**
20 minutes

**COOK TIME**
1 hour

**SERVES**
8

The Discada Norteña is one of those *wow* kind of outdoor cooks that puts on a show while delivering a uniquely delicious dish, thanks to the flavorful mix of five kinds of meat and vegetables. This recipe requires a *disco*, which can be found online.

★ ★ ★

1 (12oz/340g) package thick-cut bacon, cut into ½-inch (1.25cm) strips

1 lb (450g) country-style boneless pork ribs, diced into 1-inch (2.5cm) pieces

1 lb (450g) fajitas (skirt steak), diced into 1-inch (2.5cm) pieces

Salt, to season

Black pepper, to season

1 chorizo link, casing removed

1 medium white onion, diced

½ medium red bell pepper, ribs and seeds removed, and diced

½ medium yellow bell pepper, ribs and seeds removed, and diced

½ medium green bell pepper, ribs and seeds removed, and diced

3 serrano chiles, diced

3 jalapeños, diced

½ lb (225g) ham steak, diced into ½-inch (1.25cm) pieces

1 Roma tomato, diced

12-oz (350ml) can beer

2 scallions, chopped

Juice of 3 or 4 limes

1 bunch of fresh cilantro, chopped

1  Heat a disco over a gas burner to medium. When it's hot, add the bacon in the center, and stir frequently as the fat renders out. Cook it until halfway cooked, 3 to 5 minutes, and then push it way up toward the outer rim of the disco and form a ring of bacon on the perimeter.

2  Next add the pork in the center, season lightly with salt and pepper, and repeat the process, cooking the pork for 15 minutes, stirring occasionally, before pushing it out toward the rim to form a second ring by the bacon.

3  Repeat with the fajitas. Season lightly with salt and pepper and cook until halfway cooked. This cooks quickly, in about 5 minutes. Push the fajitas up into a third ring when they are halfway cooked.

4  Add the chorizo, mash and cook until it is fully broken up, about 3 to 5 minutes. Then push it up to create another ring.

5  Drop the onion and bell peppers in the center, and repeat the process, stirring for 2 or 3 minutes before creating the next ring. Repeat the process again with the serranos and jalapeños, cooking for 2 minutes before creating another ring.

6  Add the ham and repeat the process, cooking for 3 to 5 minutes before pushing it out when mostly cooked. By this point, you should have just the right amount of fat still left in the disco to finish cooking.

7  Finally, add the tomato to the center and begin moving down all the rings and incorporating the ingredients. Pour the beer around the dish, and bring the heat up to medium-high for a low simmer.

8  When simmering, add the scallions, lime juice, and cilantro, and simmer for 5 to 10 minutes to finish cooking. Reduce the heat to low to keep warm, and serve from the disco.

# TEXAS CHILI

**PREP TIME**
20 minutes

**COOK TIME**
3 hours

**SERVES**
10

This is my award-winning chili recipe, perfected after decades of experimenting. Many cook-off judges have honored this recipe over the years, but the most important accolades I've received have come from friends and family, who love this Texas bowl of red.

2 tbsp cooking oil, divided

3 lb (1.35kg) ground beef

¼ cup beef broth

½ medium white onion, diced

1 green bell pepper, ribs and seeds removed, and finely diced

5 garlic cloves, minced

3 Roma tomatoes, diced

¼ cup tomato paste

2 tbsp Worcestershire sauce

1 tbsp beef bouillon

2 tbsp all-purpose flour

**SEASONING BLEND**

4 tbsp chili powder

2 tbsp smoked paprika

½ tsp dried Mexican oregano

2 tsp ground cumin

1 tsp cayenne

1 tbsp salt

1 tsp black pepper

**MIREPOIX**

2 tbsp salted butter

½ cup diced white onion

½ cup diced carrots

¼ cup diced celery

**1** Make the seasoning blend: Mix the chili powder, paprika, oregano, cumin, cayenne, salt, and black pepper in a small bowl. Set aside.

**2** Heat a 12-inch (30.5cm) skillet over medium-high heat, and add 1 tablespoon of oil. Add half of the ground beef and begin to brown. When browned, transfer it to an 8-quart (7.5-liter) stockpot.

**3** Add the beef broth to the skillet to loosen the fond. When the fond has loosened and the broth has mostly evaporated, add the remaining ground beef, brown, and transfer to the stockpot.

**4** Reduce the heat under the skillet to medium, and add the remaining 1 tablespoon of oil. Add the onion, and sauté for 2 minutes. Add the bell pepper, and sauté for 1 minute. Add the garlic, and sauté for 1 minute. Add the tomatoes and tomato paste, and sauté for 2 minutes. Add the Worcestershire sauce and beef bouillon. Stir to incorporate thoroughly then transfer the vegetables to the stockpot.

**5** Set the stockpot over medium heat, and add the seasoning blend. Fill the pot with enough water to cover the ingredients by 1 to 2 inches (2.5–5cm). Bring to a boil, then reduce the heat to low, and maintain a simmer.

**6** Make the mirepoix: Set the skillet over medium heat, and add the butter. When melted, add the onion, carrots, and celery. Reduce the heat to low, and sauté, stirring frequently, for 8 to 10 minutes. Do not burn or toast the vegetables. When the vegetables are completely soft, transfer them to the stockpot. Cook the chili at a low simmer for 2 hours.

7　Heat a small skillet over medium heat, and add the flour. Toast the flour, stirring frequently, just until lightly golden. Transfer it to a small bowl and let cool for about 5 minutes. Add ¼ cup of cool water to the flour, and stir until well combined. Stir the flour mixture into the chili during the last 30 minutes of cooking time.

8　After 2 hours, turn off the heat, and let the chili cool for 15 minutes before serving.

## PRO TIPS

*You'll notice that this recipe does not contain pinto beans. That's not because I take the side of the argument that claims beans do not belong in chili. Rather, I prefer to add a few tablespoons of my Basic Beans—Traditional (page 204) to my bowl of chili to get the best of both worlds. For more spice and heat, you can add 1 or 2 tablespoons of Salsa Verde—Base (page 40) to individual bowls when serving, or double the amount of cayenne. You also can serve with fresh diced jalapeños, serranos, habaneros, or piquíns for a boost of heat.*

*I like to use Better Than Bouillon Roasted Beef Base for this recipe, because it contains potato starch that helps thicken the chili, but you can also use granulated bouillon or bouillon paste.*

# MENUDO

**PREP TIME**
30 minutes

**COOK TIME**
6 to 8 hours

**SERVES**
15

This traditional, richly flavored soup is made with beef tripe and chiles and is another definitive dish of South Texas with roots in Mexican cuisine. Plenty of restaurants and families regularly serve it, especially on the weekends, when it is side by side with barbacoa at every tortilleria, meat market, and panadería. In my family, we jokingly say that this recipe, "Esta tan sabroso que revive muertos" —meaning that the menudo could revive the dead, which is just a fun way of saying it's a great way to nurse a hangover. But I digress. This is my mother's go-to recipe, and it has since become mine, too. I hope you love it just the same.

8 lb (3.5kg) beef tripe

2 pieces pork feet (optional)

4½ cups Chile Guajillo Sauce (page 56)

4 tsp dried Mexican oregano

3 tsp ground cumin

2 tbsp salt

4 cups hominy, drained

Corn tortillas

Fresh chopped cilantro

Diced white onion

Diced jalapeños

Lime wedges

1   Rinse the beef tripe very thoroughly. Repeat at least 3 to 5 times. Cut the tripe into approximately 1-inch (2.5cm) squares, and rinse it one more time.

2   Add the beef tripe and pork feet (if using) to a large stockpot, and add water to cover by 2 inches (5cm). Set over medium heat, and simmer for 3 hours.

3   At the 3-hour mark, add the Chile Guajillo Sauce, oregano, cumin, and salt. Stir, and cook for another 2 hours.

4   At the 5-hour mark, the tripe should be fully cooked. Taste it for texture; it should be very soft without any need for excessive chewing. If it's not quite there, let it cook for an additional 1 to 3 hours, until the meat is very tender.

5   Once the tripe is fully tender, add the hominy and cook for 30 minutes. Turn off the heat. Taste and add additional salt, if needed.

6   Serve in bowls, topped with cilantro, onions, jalapeños, and a squeeze of lime, and corn tortillas on the side.

# PARRILLADA

**PREP TIME**
30 minutes

**COOK TIME**
1½ hours

**SERVES**
10 to 12

This is the perfect family-style spread for a carne asada. This is a slightly advanced cook because it requires fire and time management to ensure all the proteins are ready to serve at the same time. (Note: This recipe is written to be cooked on a kettle-style grill. You can adjust this recipe as needed to accommodate your preferred grill.)

★ ★ ★

⅓ cup ArnieTex Beef Seasoning Blend (page 25)

2 lb (1kg) tablitas, cut ¼ to ⅜ inch (6mm–1cm) thick

2 lb (1kg) chicken fajitas

2 lb (1kg) beef fajitas

2 sausage links

10 jalapeños

1 Apply ArnieTex Beef Seasoning Blend generously all over the tablitas, chicken fajitas, and beef fajitas. Set aside.

2 With one full, lit chimney of charcoal, arrange the grill's fire for dual-zone cooking and set the cooking temperature for 275°F to 300°F (140°C to 150°C).

3 Lay the tablitas directly over the fire. Cook, flipping about every 2 minutes, to develop char and color. If your fire is flaring up, cover the grill with the lid to stop it. After about 7 minutes of developing color, move the tablitas to indirect heat.

4 Next, cook the chicken fajitas in the same way and then move them to indirect heat with the tablitas. While the chicken is cooking, add the sausage links and jalapeños to the grill over indirect heat, and cook, flipping and rotating, for about 5 minutes.

5 Remove the tablitas from the grill, wrap tightly in foil, and return them to the grill over indirect heat to continue cooking. Remove the chicken fajitas from the grill, wrap tightly in foil, and return to the grill over indirect heat. Cook the wrapped tablitas and chicken for 30 to 45 minutes.

6 Meanwhile, move the sausages to direct heat to develop char by flipping and rotating them for about 3 to 5 minutes, depending on the heat. Remove from the grill, wrap in foil, and return to indirect heat. The tablitas, chicken fajitas, and sausages are now all wrapped in foil and over indirect heat, and the jalapeños are unwrapped over indirect heat. Leave the lid off the grill for 3 to 5 minutes— enough time for the coals to reheat fully. You want them to be as hot as possible.

7 Add the beef fajitas to the grill over direct heat, and cook, flipping every 3 or 4 minutes, until they develop a nice char and color. Remove the beef fajitas from the heat when they reach an internal temperature of 140°F (60°C) degrees for medium, or at your preferred doneness. If the fire flares too much, move the fajitas to indirect heat, add the lid, and let them finish cooking on indirect heat, flipping every 2 or 3 minutes.

8 Remove the beef fajitas from the grill, wrap tightly in foil, and set aside. Remove the other meats and the jalapeños from the grill, and set aside to rest for 10 to 15 minutes. Slice the beef and chicken fajitas against the grain into ½-inch (1.25cm) strips. Slice the sausage into ½-inch (1.25cm) slices, and cut the tablitas in half. Serve with MommaTex's Mexican Rice (page 207), Charro Beans (page 202), Fire-Roasted Salsa (page 48), Guacamole (page 208), and tortillas.

PREP TIME
15 minutes

COOK TIME
40 minutes

SERVES
5 or 6

# DOVE POPPERS

For a few weeks every year, we have the opportunity to hunt doves in South Texas. I did this often when I was younger yet moved away from it as the years went by. Recently, I was able to attend opening day at my good friend Jaime Perez's ranch, where I was treated to this dish. Memories came flooding back in a burst of flavor. This recipe, also called "birds on a roost," carries a massive amount of culture and stories and must continue to be passed to the next generation. In addition to being regionally specific, this recipe requires either hunting doves yourself or being lucky enough to have a friend willing to share.

★  ★

20 dove breasts

½ cup ArnieTex Pork Seasoning Blend (page 25), plus more as needed

16 oz (450g) cream cheese

1 red onion, sliced into ½-inch (1.25cm) strips

2 red bell peppers, ribs and seeds removed, and sliced into ½-inch (1.25cm) strips

5 jalapeños, sliced into ½-inch (1.25cm) strips (optional)

20 slices of bacon

1½ cups your favorite barbecue sauce, plus more as needed

Skewers

1   With one full, lit chimney of charcoal, arrange the grill's fire for dual-zone cooking and set the cooking temperature for 275°F (140°C).

2   Remove the rib cages and breast plates from the doves, forming butterflied breasts. Do not separate the breasts. Lay the breasts out open on a cutting board or clean work surface, and season with the ArnieTex Pork Seasoning Blend.

3   Add about 1 tablespoon of cream cheese on top of each open breast, followed by 1 strip of onion, bell pepper, and jalapeño.

4   Carefully close the breast, holding all the ingredients inside. Tightly wrap 1 strip of bacon around the stuffed breast. While still holding the stuffed breast, run a bamboo skewer through it to hold the bacon around the breast. Repeat this process for the remaining breasts, forming skewers of 3 to 5 doves each, spaced ¼ to ½ inch (0.5–1.25cm) apart for even cooking. (For added security and easier mobility on the grill, you can run 2 skewers through the breasts.) Lightly season the exteriors of the breasts with more of the seasoning blend.

5   Lay the skewers on the grill's indirect heat, and close the lid. At the 20-minute mark, rotate the skewers to ensure even cooking and color developing on all sides. Close the lid, and cook for 10 more minutes. Check the temperature with a meat thermometer. When the internal temperature reads 150°F (65°C), move the skewers directly over the coals to begin crisping the bacon. Cook, rotating every minute to ensure even cooking on all sides, for 5 minutes.

6   Transfer the skewers to indirect heat, and lightly baste them with the barbecue sauce. Close the lid and allow the sauce to set for 3 to 5 minutes. Check the temperature once more; the birds are fully cooked and ready to serve when they hit 165°F (75°C). You can apply another layer of barbecue sauce baste at this time if you like.

7   Remove from the grill, and serve warm.

# FIDEO

I have great memories from growing up on a farm. I'd spend long afternoons having fun in the sun with the other kids there, playing tag and hide-and-seek and swimming in the canals. I have a distinct recollection of one day, when I returned home soaking wet from swimming in the canal and sat down to a big bowl of warm fideo. I can still taste that flavorful bowl of fideo, and this is that recipe.

★ ★ ★

2 tbsp cooking oil

5-oz (140g) box of vermicelli noodles

¼ medium white onion, thinly sliced

1 garlic clove, diced

1 Roma tomato, quartered

¼ medium green bell pepper, ribs and seeds removed, and diced

½ tsp salt

1 dash of black pepper

¼ tsp ground cumin

¼ cup tomato sauce

4 cups chicken broth

1 tbsp of chopped fresh cilantro leaves

1 Heat a 12-inch (30.5cm) skillet set over medium-high heat, and add the oil. When the oil is hot, add the vermicelli (fideo), and stir frequently as it begins to brown, 3 to 4 minutes.

2 Add the onions, and stir for 2 minutes.

3 At this point, the fideo should have a nice golden-brown color. Add the garlic, tomato, bell pepper, salt, pepper, and cumin, and stir for 30 seconds.

4 Add the tomato sauce and chicken broth to completely cover the ingredients. Reduce the heat to medium, cover, and simmer for 15 minutes.

5 Turn off the heat, add the cilantro, and let cool for 5 minutes. Serve in a bowl.

## COOKING NOTES

*I love to eat this by putting some Basic Beans—Traditional (page 204) directly into the bowl of fideo along with some Pico de Gallo (page 34).*

# SMOKED BARBACOA

**PREP TIME**
15 minutes plus 30 minutes to rest

**COOK TIME**
5 hours

**SERVES**
10

On the ranch, my father often made barbacoa the traditional way—en pozo. This would be a 4-foot (1.2m) hole with a base of red-hot coals, in which he would lower in an entire cabeza (cow's head) that had been seasoned and wrapped in wet burlap sacks. He'd cover and seal the hole overnight, and the next morning, we would have perfect barbacoa de cabeza. This recipe is much more accessible and packs in all the familiar delicious flavor. Rather than a pozo and raging bed of coals, it uses your barbecue smoker or grill.

6 lb (2.75kg) cachete (beef cheek meat)

3 lb (1.35kg) lengua (beef tongue)

1 tbsp salt

2 tsp black pepper

Wood chunks or chips (your preferred wood; optional)

1 medium white onion, sliced

5 garlic cloves

1 bay leaf

2 cups beef broth

20 tortillas

1 medium onion, diced

1 bunch of fresh cilantro, diced

Salsa (your favorite)

1  Rinse the cachete, and transfer to a cutting board. Remove and discard any large chunks of fat.

2  Rinse the lengua thoroughly. (No need to trim it.)

3  Season the meats with salt and pepper. Set aside to allow the seasoning to absorb while you light the fire.

4  Set the cooking temperature on your barbecue smoker or grill to 250°F (120°C). For added smoke flavor, add the wood chunks or chips (if using).

5  Place the meats directly onto the grates in an indirect cooking zone, and smoke for 2 hours.

6  Transfer the meat to a 9 × 13-inch (23 × 33cm) baking pan or disposable aluminum pan. Add the onion, garlic, bay leaf, and beef broth. Cover tightly with double layers of aluminum foil, and return the pan to the cooker for 3 more hours.

7  At the 5-hour mark, check for doneness with a meat thermometer; the meat should be between 200°F and 205°F (95°C and 97°C) in the thickest part. It should be fork-tender and soft enough to fall apart if pulled with tongs. If not, cover and cook for 1 to 3 more hours, checking it every hour, until it is fall-apart tender.

8  Allow the meat to rest, covered, for 30 minutes and then remove the foil. Pull apart the cachete with forks or tongs, and transfer it to a warming pan. Next, peel the skin off the lengua and discard it. Finely chop the lengua, and transfer it to the warming pan. Mix thoroughly with the cachete.

9  Serve the meats with tortillas, diced onions and cilantro to garnish, and your favorite salsa.

# BIRRIA DE RES

**PREP TIME**
30 minutes

**COOK TIME**
4 ½ hours

**SERVES**
8

Originating in the Mexican state of Jalisco, birria has taken the world by storm, evolving from its natural form of tacos into birria pizza, birria ramen, and more. It's traditional to use goat for this recipe, but the accessibility of beef has made it the first choice for most people when cooking this dish.

★ ★ ★

- 4 tbsp plus ½ cup avocado oil, divided
- 3 lb (1.35kg) chuck, cut into 1½- to 2-inch (3.75 to 5cm) pieces
- 4 cups beef broth, divided
- 1½ tsp dried Mexican oregano
- 3 tsp ground cumin
- 2 tbsp salt
- 1 tsp black pepper
- 1 bay leaf

- 24 corn tortillas
- 1 bunch of fresh cilantro, chopped
- 1 medium white onion, diced
- 4 limes, quartered

### CHILE SAUCE

- 9 chiles guajillo, stems and seeds removed
- 3 chiles ancho, stems and seeds removed

- 2 chiles pasilla, stems and seeds removed
- 3 chiles de árbol
- 5 garlic cloves
- 1 medium white onion, quartered
- 5 Roma tomatoes
- ½ cinnamon stick
- 2 whole cloves

1  To make the chile sauce, rinse the chiles guajillo, ancho, pasilla, and de árbol under cold water.

2  Add 6 cups of water to a 4-quart (3.8-liter) stockpot, set over medium-high heat, and bring to a slow boil. Reduce the heat to medium-low, and bring to a low simmer. Add the chiles, garlic, quartered onion, tomatoes, cinnamon stick, and cloves, and simmer for 10 minutes. Turn off the heat, and allow the ingredients to stand in the water for 5 minutes.

3  Transfer all the ingredients, along with the cooking water, to a large blender, and blend on high for 90 seconds. (If you need to, you can do this in batches.) Strain the sauce through a sieve back into the stockpot. Use the back of a spoon or a spatula to press all the liquid through the sieve. Set aside the chile sauce.

4  Set an 8-quart (7.5-liter) stockpot over medium-high heat, and add 2 tablespoons of avocado oil. Add half of the chuck, and sear for about 3 to 5 minutes per side. Transfer the seared chuck to a large bowl.

5  Add ½ cup of beef broth to the stockpot, and begin to lift the fond from the bottom of the pot. Pour the fond and beef broth into the bowl.

6  Add 2 tablespoons of avocado oil to the stockpot, and sear the remaining chuck. Transfer the meat to the bowl. Add ½ cup of beef broth to the pot, lift the fond from the bottom of pot again, and then transfer to the bowl.

7  Set the 8-quart (7.5-liter) stockpot over medium-high heat, and add the remaining ½ cup of avocado oil. When the oil is hot, add the chile sauce along with the oregano, cumin, salt, pepper, and bay leaf. Reduce the heat to medium-low, and simmer, stirring every 2 minutes, for 10 minutes.

8   Add the seared chuck, fond, and broth from the bowl to the stockpot, along with the remaining 3 cups of beef broth. Increase the heat to medium-high, and bring to a boil. Reduce the heat to medium-low, and slow boil for 3½ hours.

9   Shut off the heat, and allow the meat to stand in the broth for 30 minutes.

10  Transfer the meat from the stockpot to a large cutting board, and roughly chop with a heavy knife. Add the meat to a 12-inch (30.5cm) skillet.

11  Add 2 cups of the consommé in the stockpot to the skillet, and toss to mix. Set over low heat to keep warm.

12  Dip each tortilla in the remaining consommé in the stockpot, place in a 10-inch (25.5cm) skillet set over medium heat, and allow the tortillas to crisp in the skillet for 2 to 4 minutes. Add about 2 tablespoons of the meat to the tortilla and fold while still in the skillet. Flip over the filled tortilla, and toast each side to your preferred doneness. Transfer to a serving plate, and repeat with the remaining tortillas and birria.

13  Serve immediately with your favorite salsa, chopped cilantro, diced onions, and lime quarters, along with ¼ to ½ cup of the consommé for dipping. (Remove the bay leaf from the consommé and discard before serving.)

## PRO TIPS

*To make these into quesabirria tacos, add 1 or 2 tablespoons of shredded Oaxaca cheese to each taco during step 12.*

# MOLLEJAS

**PREP TIME**
10 minutes

**COOK TIME**
2 hours

**SERVES**
4

Mollejas, also known as sweetbreads, are a delicacy in Mexican culture. Their popularity is so great that you often can find them as a protein option at local taquerias. When cooked perfectly, their taste and texture are incredible. I like to cook them on the grill for maximum flavor.

★ ★ ★

2 lb (1kg) mollejas (sweetbreads)

¼ cup ArnieTex Beef Seasoning Blend (page 25)

Wood chunks or chips (your preferred wood; optional)

2 tbsp cooking oil

1 tbsp salted butter

Corn tortillas, warmed

½ cup chopped fresh cilantro

½ diced medium white onion

2 limes, quartered

Pico de Gallo (page 34) or your favorite salsa

1  Rinse the mollejas thoroughly in cold water. Trim off any large, hard pieces of fat.

2  Season all sides of the mollejas with a medium coat of ArnieTex Beef Seasoning Blend, and set aside.

3  With one full, lit chimney of charcoal, arrange the grill's fire for dual-zone cooking and set the cooking temperature for 250°F to 275°F (120°C to 140°C). For added smoke and flavor, add the wood chunks (if using) to the coals, ensuring that they are lit and emitting a thin blue or translucent smoke.

4  Lightly oil the cooking grates, and lay the mollejas directly over the coals. Cover the grill, and cook, uncovering and flipping the mollejas every 10 minutes for the next 40 minutes, re-covering after each flip and maintaining the cooking temperature. At this point, the meat should have a nice sear developing on both sides.

5  Stack two long pieces of foil. Transfer the mollejas to the foil, and set the butter on top. Wrap the mollejas tightly in the foil, and return to grill away from the direct coals. Cook indirectly for 1 hour. At the 30-minute mark, rotate the mollejas 180 degrees to allow for even cooking.

6  After 1 hour, remove the wrapped mollejas from the grill. Set on a baking sheet or in an aluminum cooking tray that will fit inside the grill. Carefully open the foil to expose the mollejas, being careful not to let any melted butter run out of the foil. Add the sheet or tray to the grill directly over the coals, and cook, flipping the mollejas every 2 minutes, until the outside color is golden brown, about 10 minutes.

7  Remove the sheet or tray from the grill, and set aside for 5 minutes.

8  Chop the mollejas into strips or bite-sized pieces. Add to the warmed tortillas to make tacos, and top with the cilantro, onion, and a lime on the side. Add some Pico de Gallo or your favorite salsa, and serve.

## PRO TIPS

*You can butterfly the mollejas after rinsing and trimming the fat to allow for more seasoning coverage and to speed up the cooking time to about twice as fast.*

# CARNITAS

**PREP TIME**
15 minutes

**COOK TIME**
2 hours

**SERVES**
8

There's more than one way to enjoy a pork butt, and carnitas is a contender for one of the best cooking methods. The delicious, crispy exterior and juicy tenderness inside are perfect for breakfast or street-style tacos at any time of the day. Because this is a somewhat involved recipe, once you master the technique, you can show it off at your next taco night to impress your friends and family.

★ ★ ★

6 lb (2.75kg) pork butt
5 lb (2.25kg) pork lard
1 medium white onion, quartered
4 garlic cloves, smashed

1 orange
2 tbsp salt
12-oz (350ml) can cola
Corn tortillas, warmed

1 medium white onion, diced
Chopped fresh cilantro
2 large avocados, peeled, pitted, and sliced
Salsa (your favorite)

1 Carve the pork butt downward into slices 2 to 3 inches (5 to 7.5cm) thick. Then, cut the slices into carnitas-sized chunks about 2 to 3 inches (5 to 7.5cm) thick. Set aside.

2 Heat a 12-quart (11.5-liter) stockpot or cazo over medium heat, and add the lard to melt. When the lard begins to simmer, carefully add the carnitas chunks to the pot and slow boil, stirring the meat up from the bottom of the pot every 5 to 7 minutes to prevent burning, for 30 minutes.

3 At the 30-minute mark, add the onion and garlic, and stir once to incorporate the ingredients.

4 Cut the orange in half, deseed, and squeeze the juice into the pot. Carefully drop the juiced halves in the pot.

5 Add 1 cup of water and the salt to a measuring cup, and stir until the salt is fully dissolved. Carefully add the salted water to the pot, and cook, stirring every 5 to 7 minutes, for 1 more hour.

6 At the 1½-hour mark, pour the cola into the pot. Cook, stirring frequently, for 30 minutes.

7 Using tongs or a spider strainer, carefully transfer the carnitas to a wire rack set on top of a baking sheet, and allow them to cool.

8 Increase the heat under the pot to medium-high, and bring the oil to 325°F to 350°F (165°C to 180°C). In two or three batches, drop the cooled carnitas into the oil and fry until they look nicely browned, 2 or 3 minutes. Transfer the carnitas to the rack, and allow to cool for 5 minutes.

9 Shred the carnitas with a fork, or chop with a knife. Serve with warm corn tortillas, diced onions and cilantro for topping, and sliced avocados and your favorite salsa on the side.

# PAN DE CAMPO

**PREP TIME**
30 minutes, plus
2 hours to rest

**COOK TIME**
20 minutes

**SERVES**
12

Pan de Campo (cowboy bread) is the official state bread of Texas for a few reasons. Its simple cooking process made it easy for the vaqueros of South Texas to prepare in Dutch ovens while on the open range. It's also a big ol' circular piece of bread, perfectly in line with everything being bigger in Texas. This is my family recipe that we have honed for years. I love to serve it with a slather of butter and drizzle of honey.

★ ★ ★

4 cups all-purpose flour, plus more for dusting

4 tbsp baking powder

3 tsp salt

3 tsp sugar

½ cup plus ½ tsp vegetable oil, divided

1½ cups buttermilk or whole milk, cooled

1. Whisk together the flour, baking powder, salt, and sugar in a large bowl.

2. Add the ½ cup of oil, and stir to incorporate evenly.

3. Add the buttermilk a little at a time while kneading the dough for about 1 minute. Do not over-knead. The dough should be tacky and without clumps. (You might not need all the buttermilk.) Cover the bowl with plastic wrap or a towel, and let rest at room temperature for 2 hours.

4. Preheat the oven to 375°F (190°C) degrees. Lightly oil a baking sheet with the remaining ½ teaspoon of oil.

5. Dust a work surface with flour. Turn out the dough, divide it into three equal portions, and pat into 8- or 9-inch (20 or 23cm) circles about ½ inch (1.25cm) thick. You also can use a rolling pin for this step.

6. Using a fork, poke several holes all over the top of each circle, and place the circles on the prepared baking sheet.

7. Bake for 15 minutes. Check the bread loaves at this point, flipping or rotating them for more even cooking as necessary. Return to the oven for 5 more minutes. The bread should have a beautifully golden-brown color on the top. Remove from the oven, and serve.

## COOKING NOTES

*Elevation, heat, and humidity can affect the bread, and the measurements may need micro-adjustments. If the dough is too firm, add a little more milk. If the bread is too thin, add a touch more flour. In both cases, be careful not to over-knead. If the oven temperature seems too hot or cool, adjust slightly as needed.*

# TAMALES

**PREP TIME**
1 hour

**COOK TIME**
4 hours,
20 minutes

**MAKES**
10 dozen

Tamales are a delicious, traditional part of Mexican cuisine that varies by region and home. Made from masa (corn dough), tamales can be filled with pork, chicken, beans, or even cream cheese with jalapeños. In my family, pork is the filling of choice, and this is the recipe handed down from generation to generation. Due to the scale of the recipe, preparation of the tamales is often a communal activity, called a tamalada, where several hundreds of tamales are made at once as family and friends gather to cook the whole day, sharing stories and carrying on the tradition. After everyone eats the fresh steamed tamales, they usually leave with as many dozens as they can carry.

★ ★ ★

### PORK BOIL
8 lb (3.5kg) pork butt, quartered

4 garlic cloves

1 medium white onion, quartered

2 tbsp salt

1 tsp black pepper

1 tsp ground cumin

Corn husks (about 150)

### CHILE SAUCE
2 tbsp lard

4 cups Chile Guajillo Sauce (page 56)

1 tsp salt

### MASA
8 cups masa harina

2 tbsp baking powder

2 cups lard, melted

4 tsp salt

### TAMALE MEAT
1 cup lard

1 tsp salt

½ tsp black pepper

1 tsp ground cumin

½ tsp dried Mexican oregano

1 Make the pork boil: Add 1 gallon (3.75 liters) of water to a 12-quart (11.5-liter) stockpot, along with the pork, garlic, onion, salt, pepper, and cumin. Set over medium-high heat, and bring to a slow boil. Reduce heat to medium-low and maintain a slow boil until the meat is fall-apart tender, about 2 hours. Turn off the heat, and let the meat cool in the water for 30 minutes. Reserve 9 cups of the pork broth. Transfer the pork to a cutting board. Debone it and then shred it.

2 While the pork is cooking, sort through the husks to ensure you have at least 130 to 140 usable ones; some may be ripped, too small, or damaged.

3 Add 8 cups of water to an 8-quart (7.5-liter) stockpot, and lay each husk in the water individually. Use a bowl or plate to weigh down the husks, ensuring all are completely submerged in the water, adding more water as needed. Soak the husks at least 2 hours to completely soften. (I recommend 4 or 5 hours.)

4 To prepare the chile sauce, heat a 10-inch (25.5cm) skillet over medium heat, and add the lard. When the lard is melted, add the Chile Guajillo Sauce and salt. Lightly pan-fry the sauce, stirring about every 30 seconds or so, for 10 minutes. (You only need about half or two-thirds of the prepared sauce for this recipe. Store the leftovers in an airtight container in the refrigerator for up to 3 days, or freeze for up to 3 months.)

5   To make the masa, whisk together the masa harina and baking powder in a large bowl. Add the melted lard and 2 cups of the prepared chili sauce from step 4. Using your hands, knead the mixture until well combined. Add the pork broth from step 1 while kneading, about ½ cup at a time, until 4 cups have been incorporated. Keep kneading until the dough is soft to the touch but not tacky. When you squeeze the dough, no bits of masa should stick to your hands or fingers. You can add more water or pork broth as you knead, about 2 tablespoons at a time, as needed.

6   To make the tamale meat, melt the lard in a 12-inch (30.5cm) skillet over medium heat. Add 1 cup of the chile sauce from step 4, along with the salt, pepper, cumin, and oregano, and stir to combine. Add half of the shredded pork to the skillet, and sauté, stirring often, for 5 minutes. Add 2½ cups of the pork broth from step 1, and cook, stirring every minute or so, for 5 more minutes. Turn off the heat, and transfer the pork to a large bowl. Repeat with the remaining pork, 1 cup more chile sauce, and 2½ cups more broth.

7   Remove the husks from the water and drain. While the husks are still wet, begin rolling the tamales. Lay one husk flat on your work surface. Using a spatula or large spoon, spread 2 tablespoons of the masa in a thin layer on the husk, starting at the wide part of the husk and spreading toward the narrow end, about 5 to 6 inches (13 to 15cm). Add 2 tablespoons of pork on the masa, and spread out the meat over the masa, leaving a ½- to ¾-inch (1.25 to 2cm) strip of masa uncovered at the top and bottom of the husk. (This will help during the rolling.) Roll the filled husk into itself by folding one long edge of the husk three-fourths of the way over the filling, so the masa folds onto itself and will bind during steaming. Fold again to seal the remaining masa to the husk, so the husk will remove easily after cooking. Finally, fold the tamale in half so the narrow end is beneath the stuffed end. Set aside and repeat with the remaining ingredients.

8   In a 10-quart (9.5-liter) steamer, add water to just below the steaming grate. Place a small, heatproof bowl inside the steamer, and stand the tamales around the bowl, folded end down. You can add two or three layers of tamales, but to avoid overcrowding the steamer, cook the tamales in batches. Cover the steamer, set over medium heat, and cook for 1 hour. Turn off the heat and let cool for 15 minutes before serving with your favorite salsas.

## PRO TIPS

*My favorite way to eat tamales is actually the next day: Heat a comal or griddle over low heat. Add the tamales, straight from the refrigerator, to the comal, and cook, rotating them every 1 or 2 minutes, until the husks begin to char and you can smell the crisp masa, at least 7 to 10 minutes and up to 15 minutes. Remove the tamales from the griddle, allow to cool for 2 minutes, then unwrap. They will have a crispy, crunchy exterior with a delicious char flavor.*

# 8
# TEJANO BAR-B-QUE

## PRO TIPS

The keys to this recipe are a steady, consistent cooking temperature and patience because pork butt can take 8, 10, or sometimes even up to 14 hours to cook. Ensure that you have plenty of cooking fuel on hand for the entire cook time. If you like, you can add a few wood chunks for added smoke and flavor during step 2, ensuring that they are lit and emitting a clear, translucent smoke. You also can omit the sugar from this recipe and use the finished pulled pork for tacos to serve with salsa.

# PULLED PORK

**PREP TIME**
20 minutes

**COOK TIME**
10 to 12 hours

**SERVES**
12 to 14

Pork butt is a wonderful hunk of meat. Made from as many as 12 to 14 muscles, this is one of the most versatile cuts of meat on any animal. Like a brisket, pork butt is simple to master with a little time, patience, and attention. And after the heat breaks down all the connective tissue, intramuscular fat, and collagen, you'll see why this meat is so beloved. Enjoy this on a sandwich with coleslaw and your favorite barbecue sauce.

9–12 lb (4–5.5kg) pork butt

¾ cup ArnieTex Pork Seasoning Blend (page 25)

¼ cup turbinado sugar

¼ cup apple cider vinegar

Wood chunks or chips (your preferred wood; optional)

4 tbsp salted butter, divided

1 cup dark brown sugar, firmly packed, divided

1  Rinse the pork butt thoroughly, and trim off any noticeable excess fat. With the meat side up, generously season with the ArnieTex Pork Seasoning Blend, ensuring that all sides are completely covered. Again with the meat side up, evenly season the entire pork butt with turbinado sugar. Set aside.

2  Prepare an indirect cook in a smoker with a cooking temperature of 250°F (120°C).

3  Place the meat on the far side of the cooker, away from the direct heat. Close the lid, set the vents to maintain 250°F (120°C), and cook for 2 hours. For added smoke and flavor, add the wood chunks (if using) to the coals, ensuring they are emitting a thin blue or translucent smoke. After 2 hours, check the meat; it should be developing a slightly darker color at this point.

4  Combine ¾ cup of water and the apple cider vinegar in a spray bottle. Evenly spritz the meat with just enough liquid to moisten the exterior of the meat. Close the lid and cook for 2 hours, spritzing every 30 minutes. After 2 hours, rotate the meat 180 degrees to ensure even color on each side. Continue spritzing and turning the meat every 2 hours until the internal temperature reaches 170°F to 175°F (77°C to 80°C). At this point, the meat should have a dark, even color. Remove from the smoker.

5  Melt 2 tablespoons of butter in a small saucepan over medium-low heat. Stack two long pieces of foil. Place the remaining 2 tablespoons of unmelted butter and ½ cup of brown sugar in the center of the foil. Set the pork butt directly on top, and baste the entire pork butt with the melted butter. Lightly season the entire pork butt with more seasoning blend and the remaining ½ cup of brown sugar. Wrap the meat tightly in the double foil, and return it to the smoker. Cook, maintaining a temperature of 250°F (120°C) degrees and checking the meat every hour, until it reaches an internal temperature of 203°F to 205°F (96°C to 97°C).

6  Remove the pork butt from the smoker, and allow it to rest for 1 to 3 hours. Unwrap it, and place it in a large pan. Preserve the juices in the pan and pour all of them into a fat separator to isolate the natural juices from the fat.

7  Pull apart and shred the meat using two forks. Place the pulled pork back into the pan and incorporate as much of the natural juices into the meat as you like. This helps create an extra boost of delicious flavor.

# TEXAS BRISKET

**PREP TIME**
25 minutes plus
2 to 3 hours to rest

**COOK TIME**
up to 14 hours

**SERVES**
12–15

People travel from all corners of the earth to stand in line in Texas—and in some cases even sleep outside overnight—just to try our legendary smoked brisket. No other barbecued meat in the United States commands that kind of dedication. It makes sense then that this recipe can be extremely intimidating for newcomers, and even when the confidence is there, it's easy to fall into the "how to properly cook a brisket" rabbit hole. This recipe might take some practice, but it's easy to master if you put in the time. Fire control, the right technique, and some patience will reward you with unmatched smoky, juicy, melt-in-your-mouth deliciousness. No barbecue sauce needed, unless you like it. (Note: If you're using a charcoal grill, you will need to add charcoal and wood chunks or chips to maintain cooking temperature throughout this recipe.)

14–16 lb (6.5–7.25kg) packer brisket

¼ cup salt

⅓ cup black pepper

2 tbsp yellow mustard, divided

¼ cup apple cider vinegar

1 Rinse the brisket thoroughly with cold water, pat dry with paper towels, and set on a cutting board. With the fat side of the brisket up, carefully trim off some of the fat, leaving a layer of fat about ⅛ to ¼ inch (0.25 to 0.5cm) thick. Flip over the brisket so it's fat side down, and trim off any excess visual fat. Focus on trimming only the excessive and large pieces of fat.

2 Mix the salt and pepper in a small bowl.

3 Evenly spread 1 tablespoon of mustard on the meat side of the brisket using your hand or a basting brush. Season generously with about a third of the salt and pepper mixture. Flip over the brisket so it's fat side up, evenly spread the remaining 1 tablespoon of mustard over the meat, and season with the remaining rub. Allow the brisket to sit while you ready the smoker.

4 Set the smoker to 250°F (120°C). For an authentic Texas-style flavor, I recommend cooking with post oak. Once the fire is lit, you will need to maintain it by adding one log at a time, allowing it to catch fire and burn into coals to continue the cooking process.

5 Place the brisket fat side up in the smoker with the thickest part toward the fire. Set the airflow to maintain a 250°F (120°C) cooking temperature. Close the lid and cook for 2 hours.

6 After 2 hours, combine ¾ cup of water and the vinegar in a spray bottle. Lightly spritz the brisket to encourage color and bark development. (Bark is the dark, flavorful crust a perfectly cooked brisket gets as it cooks.) Close the lid and maintain the cooking temperature for 6 more hours, spritzing at each hour mark.

7 At the 8-hour mark, check the temperature of the brisket with a meat thermometer. When it reaches 170°F to 175°F (77°C to 80°C) internal temperature, place a large sheet of butcher paper on a table or countertop. Remove the brisket from the smoker and place it on one end of the paper with the fat side

facing up. Begin to fold the paper around the brisket, folding the sides up as you go so that upon completion of the wrap, the meat side is facing down and the folds of the paper are also down. This will leave the fat side still facing up.

8  Return the brisket to the smoker with the flat muscle facing the heat. Close the lid and cook, maintaining the cooking temperature at 250°F (120°C), for 2 hours.

9  Rotate the brisket 180 degrees. The thicker point should now be facing the heat source and will remain so for the rest of the cook. Close the lid and cook, maintaining the cooking temperature, and checking the brisket's internal temperature every 30 minutes, until it reaches 203°F to 205°F (96°C to 97°C) at the thickest point. This could take between 1 and 5 hours. When checking for temperature, the thermometer probe should slide in easily as if into soft butter.

10  Remove the brisket from the smoker, and allow it to sit on a counter for 20 minutes to stop the cooking process.

11  Place the brisket in a cooler or a turned-off oven until the internal temperature drops to 160°F (70°C), about 2 or 3 hours. This is the ideal slicing and serving temperature.

12  Unwrap the brisket from the butcher paper, and slice against the grain into about ¼-inch (0.5cm) slices. Serve with your favorite barbecue sides or between two slices of white bread and drizzled with barbecue sauce.

## PRO TIPS

*A packer brisket is a whole, untrimmed brisket that contains both the flat and point muscles of the cow and can range from 11 to 20 pounds (5 to 9kg). When shopping for your packer brisket, I recommend purchasing a USDA Prime grade, which will have great marbling and intermuscular fat. A USDA Choice grade brisket is also a great option if you prefer a more affordable and slightly leaner option.*

## PRO TIPS

*Pork spare ribs come with the extra breast bone and extra meat on the knuckle side. If you prefer to avoid the trimming, you can use St. Louis spare ribs instead.*

*It is not necessary to remove the membrane on the bone side, but it's traditional for most barbecue cooks to do so. Try it both ways and see what you prefer.*

# TEXAS PORK RIBS
## [ARNIE STYLE]

Few meats are able to sustain as much marketability as pork spare ribs—even to the point that entire franchises, barbecue houses, and cook-offs are built entirely around them. This is with good reason because their large, meaty bite, combined with flavorful fat, offer one of the most delicious bites in barbecue.

★ ★ ★

1 full rack pork spare ribs (about 4 lb/2kg)

2 tbsp mustard, divided

¼ cup ArnieTex Pork Seasoning Blend (page 25)

Wood chunks or chips (your preferred wood; optional)

¼ cup apple cider vinegar

½ cup barbecue sauce, divided, plus more for serving

1 Working the ribs bone side up, on the knuckle side, use a sharp knife to trim off the extra breast bone and extra meat. Using a paper towel for grip, grab a corner of the membrane and pull it off, across the back of the ribs. Flip over the ribs, and trim off any excess fat. Rinse the ribs thoroughly, and completely pat dry with paper towels.

2 With the bone side up, evenly slather about 1 tablespoon of mustard over the meat and then generously season with the ArnieTex Pork Seasoning Blend. Set aside for 10 minutes.

3 Flip the ribs to bone side down and repeat with the remaining mustard and more seasoning blend. Set aside.

4 With one full, lit chimney of charcoal, arrange the grill's fire for dual-zone cooking and set the cooking temperature for 275°F (140°C). For added smoke and flavor, add the wood chunks (if using) to the coals, ensuring that they are emitting a thin blue or translucent smoke.

5 Set the ribs, meat side up, over indirect heat. Close the lid, and cook for 1 hour.

6 Combine ¾ cup of water and the apple cider vinegar in a spray bottle. Evenly spritz the meat with just enough liquid to moisten the exterior of the meat. Close the lid, and cook for 30 minutes. Repeat the spritzing every 30 minutes for the next 2 hours.

7 At the 3-hour mark, stack two long pieces of foil. Drizzle ¼ cup of barbecue sauce on the bottom of the foil equal to about the length of the ribs. Place the ribs, meat side down, on top of the sauce. Brush the remaining ¼ cup of barbecue sauce on the bone side and then tightly wrap the ribs in the foil.

8 Set the ribs back on the grill over the indirect heat, and maintain the 275°F (140°C) cooking temperature for 1 more hour.

9 The ribs are ready when they are probe-tender and 200°F (95°C) on a meat thermometer in the thickest part. Remove from the grill, and allow to rest, wrapped, for 15 minutes.

10 Unwrap the ribs, slice between the bones, and serve with a side of your favorite barbecue sauce.

PREP TIME
10 minutes plus
overnight to
marinate

COOK TIME
2 hours,
40 minutes

SERVES
4 to 6

# PORK BELLY CHICHARRÓN

There are levels to a fried pork skin. The ones we usually encounter first in life are the snack-sized bags with light, airy, crunchy pork skins. Later we might come across pork cracklings, which have a bit of fat and meat along with the skin. And if you're lucky, at some point you might try something like this pork belly chicharrón, which has a tremendously crunchy skin and a layer of rich, delicious fat along with juicy, tender meat. It's a bite made in heaven, and it's so simple to cook, too. Dunk these chicharrónes in your favorite salsa, use them to scoop up some Guacamole (page 208), or fill a taco with them. You might never go back to those snack-sized bags!

★ ★ ★

3 lb (1.35kg) pork belly, skin on

2 tbsp ArnieTex Pork Blend Seasoning (page 25)

½ cup salt

Wood chunks (your preferred wood; optional)

1   Place the pork belly on a cutting board, meat side up, and pat dry thoroughly with paper towels. Lightly season the meat side with the ArnieTex Pork Blend Seasoning and allow to set for 5 minutes.

2   Flip over the pork belly. Using a chef knife, carefully scrape the skin and then wipe the knife clean with a paper towel. Repeat this step up to five times to dry out the skin as much as possible.

3   Run the knife from the top of the skin to the bottom to score the skin at every 1 inch (2.5cm). Be sure the cuts do not penetrate into the meat; you only want to slice the skin.

4   Transfer the pork belly to a half cooling rack resting on a half-sheet pan, skin side up. Sprinkle the salt all over the skin, being careful not to lose any salt off the sides. The salt should form a somewhat thick layer over the entire skin side of the meat. Set the meat in the refrigerator overnight or for at least 6 or 7 hours before cooking.

5   When you're ready to cook, remove the pork belly from the refrigerator while you light the grill.

6   With one full, lit chimney of charcoal, arrange the grill's fire for dual-zone cooking and set the cooking temperature for 300°F to 325°F (150°C to 163°C). For added smoke and flavor, add the wood chunks (if using) to the coals, ensuring they are emitting a thin blue or translucent smoke.

7   Place the pork belly, still on the rack and pan, on the grill over indirect heat. Close the lid and maintain the cooking temperature of 300°F to 325°F (150°C to 163°C).

8   During the first 2 hours, every 30 minutes, open the lid and rotate the pork belly 180 degrees to encourage even cooking.

9  At the 2-hour mark, check the internal temperature using a meat thermometer. When the pork belly reaches 185°F to 190°F (85°C to 88°C), remove it from the grill and leave the lid open. If the pork belly has not reached 185°F to 190°F (85°C to 88°C), continue cooking, rotating, and checking the temperature every 30 minutes.

10  With the pork belly out of the grill and the lid open, bring the temperature of the grill grates up to 450°F to 500°F (230°C to 260°C). (Note that with the lid open, the grill temperature itself won't register 450°F/230°C so you'll have to use an infrared thermometer to check the grate temperature.)

11  As the fire is coming up in temperature, using a chef knife, scrape off all the salt from the pork belly. It should fall right off.

12  When the coals are glowing red and the cook temperature is at least 450°F (230°C), place the pork belly back on the grill over indirect heat, and close the lid. Check every minute and rotate 180 degrees each time, until the skin forms a fluffy, blistered bark, about 5 or 6 minutes. Remove the pork belly from the grill, and allow it to rest for 10 minutes.

13  Slice the pork belly from the top to the bottom, following the score lines. Then slice from left to right in your desired size, depending on if you are stuffing it into tacos, using it to dip into guacamole or salsa, or simply enjoying it as finger food.

# SMOKED TURKEY BREAST

**PREP TIME**
10 minutes plus 30 minutes to rest

**COOK TIME**
3 hours

**SERVES**
6

In Texas barbecue joints, a smoky, buttery, juicy slice of turkey breast can be just as good as any other barbecued meat, thanks to a great cooking technique and a solid recipe, both of which you will find here. Because it is a poultry breast, you will need to cook it just right, wrapping it at the correct time and with some butter for best results. Pull it at the ideal temperature, and you'll have a delicious, golden-brown turkey breast that's bursting with flavor.

4–5 lb (2–2.25kg) boneless turkey breast

1 tbsp olive oil

4 tbsp ArnieTex Poultry Seasoning Blend (page 25)

¼ cup apple cider vinegar

8 tbsp salted butter, divided

1   Rinse the turkey breast with cold water, and pat dry with paper towels. Rub the oil entirely over the turkey, and season the turkey on all sides with the ArnieTex Poultry Seasoning Blend.

2   Combine ¾ cup of water and the vinegar in a spray bottle. Set aside.

3   With one full, lit chimney of charcoal, arrange a kettle-style grill's fire for dual-zone cooking and set the cooking temperature for 275°F (140°C).

4   Place the turkey on the grill, over indirect heat, as far as possible from the heat source. Close the lid and smoke for 1 hour, spritzing at the 30 minute and 1 hour marks. Also at the 1-hour mark, rotate the turkey 180 degress. Ensure that the cooking temperature is 275°F (140°C), close the lid, and continue cooking. Spritz again every 30 minutes for the next hour.

5   At the 2-hour mark, check the internal temperature at the thickest part of the breast with a meat thermometer. When the turkey reaches 140°F (60°C) to 145°F (63°C), it's time to wrap.

6   Place 4 tablespoons of butter in a small heatproof pan over low heat on the grill or on the stove over medium heat, and melt it.

7   Lay out two strips of foil. Remove the turkey from the grill, and set it in the middle of the foil. Drizzle the butter over the top, and wrap the foil tightly around the turkey. Return the turkey to the grill and cook for 30 minutes, maintaining a cooking temperature of 275°F (140°C).

8   At the 1-hour mark, check the temperature again. Remove the turkey from the grill when it reaches 160°F to 163°F (70°C to 73°C). The carry-over cooking will take it to 165°F (75°C). Place the turkey in a turned-off oven or a cooler for 30 minutes.

9   Right before slicing the turkey, melt the remaining 4 tablespoons of butter in the pot over low heat.

10  Transfer the turkey to a cutting board, and slice across the breast. Drizzle the melted butter and any natural juices from the foil over the sliced turkey, and serve immediately.

# GRILLED CHICKEN THIGHS
## [TWO WAYS]

Chicken thighs are a solid choice for grilling due to their fat content, which means more flavor, more moisture, and more forgiveness if you cook them a few degrees beyond the usual poultry recommendation of 165°F (75°C). Bone-in chicken thighs make a great presentation piece to add to a spread of food. Boneless chicken thighs are nice for slicing and stuffing into tacos alongside other proteins or with guacamole and salsa.

★ ★ ★

12 boneless or bone-in chicken thighs

ArnieTex Poultry Seasoning Blend (page 25)

### BONELESS CHICKEN THIGHS

1  Moderately season both sides of the boneless chicken thighs with the ArnieTex Poultry Seasoning Blend.

2  With one full, lit chimney of charcoal, arrange the grill's fire for dual-zone cooking and set the cooking temperature for 300°F to 350°F (150°C to 180°C).

3  Place the thighs on the grill directly over the coals, and close the lid.

4  After 10 minutes, open the lid and flip over the thighs. Check the thighs; you're looking for a golden-brown color. Flip over the thighs again as the flames start to pop up. Keep flipping regularly, with the thighs directly over the fire, about every minute or 2 for 10 minutes. If the fire begins to get too much, close the lid for 1 minute to calm it down or move the thighs to indirect heat once you have some nice color and char.

5  Check for doneness with a meat thermometer; the chicken thighs should be between 165°F and 180°F (75°C and 82°C) in the thickest part. Remove from the grill, wrap loosely in foil, and let rest for 10 minutes before serving.

### BONE-IN CHICKEN THIGHS

1  Pull the skin back on the thighs, and moderately season the meat with the ArnieTex Poultry Seasoning Blend, folding the skin back over and under when finished. Flip over the thighs, and season the bottom. Flip again to skin side up, and season the skin.

2  With one full, lit chimney of charcoal, arrange the grill's fire for dual-zone cooking and set the cooking temperature for 275°F to 300°F (140°C to 150°C). Place the thighs on the grill directly over the coals, close the lid, and cook for 35 minutes.

3  Check for doneness with a meat thermometer; the thighs should be between 165°F and 180°F (75°C and 82°C) at the thickest part.

4  When the thighs are almost done cooking, flip them over, skin side down, and close the lid for 5 to 10 minutes. This will create a crispy, tasty skin that adds a great layer of texture and flavor to the recipe. Remove from the grill, and let rest for 10 minutes before serving.

**PREP TIME**
15 minutes

**COOK TIME**
45 minutes

**SERVES**
4 to 7

# GRILLED CHICKEN LEG QUARTERS

The leg quarter is a great cut of chicken because it packs a hearty serving of thigh and drumstick. It is also one of the stars on a perfect plate of carne asada. These cuts are also ideal for grilling in large quantities, debone, and use in other recipes such as enchiladas, flautas, tostadas, and even a chicken salad with a kick. I love to cook these right over the coals for the most delicious result. This recipe can be the epitome of "set it and forget it" because it is so easy to cook.

★ ★ ★

| 7 chicken leg quarters | ArnieTex Poultry Seasoning Blend (page 25) | Wood chunks or chips (your preferred wood; optional) |

1 Trim any excess and obvious fat from the chicken. Leaving a little is fine because it will atomize as it drips onto the hot coals, creating another layer of flavor.

2 Pull the skin back from the meat, and moderately season the meat with the ArnieTex Poultry Seasoning Blend. Place the skin back, flip over the quarters, skin side down, and season the bottom side. Allow the seasoning to set for 10 minutes. Flip over the quarters again, skin side up, and season the skin.

3 Preheat the grill to 250°F (120°C).

4 Place the chicken on the grill, skin side up, directly over the coals, and close the lid. Depending on your cooker, you should be able to let the grill cook for 30 to 45 minutes. If your fire is too hot, the skin will pull back too quickly, so be sure to stay between 250°F to 275°F (120°C to 140°C). For added smoke and flavor, add the wood chunks or chips (if using) to the coals, ensuring that they are emitting a thin blue or translucent smoke.

5 Check for doneness with a meat thermometer; the chicken should be 175°F (80°C) at the bone.

6 Remove the chicken from the grill, and let rest for up to 5 minutes before serving.

## PRO TIPS

*Serve with your favorite barbecue sides and warm flour tortillas, or glaze with your favorite barbecue sauce.*

# TEXAS CHICKEN HALVES

**PREP TIME**
20 minutes plus
10 minutes to rest

**COOK TIME**
1 hour

**SERVES**
6

Chicken halves are a favorite of mine. You get the thigh, drumstick, wing, and breast, all in one. And a good, delicious grilled chicken half reminds me of my barbecue competition days, traveling around Texas. My chicken half turn-ins were very consistent and many times helped me to walk the stages and win multiple grand championships across Texas. Because of my nostalgia, I enjoy splitting my own chickens as part of the process. You can ask your butcher to do this step if you prefer.

2 (3- to 4-lb/1.35 to 2kg) whole chickens

2 tbsp olive oil

ArnieTex Poultry Seasoning Blend (page 25)

Wood chunks or chips (your preferred wood; optional)

1   Using a pair of poultry shears, cut out the chicken's backbone. Place a sharp, heavy knife in the middle of the breast section and give it a quick, firm push with your other hand. The chicken will split in two. (One of the halves will not have the breastbone holding the breast in place, but it will cook just fine.) Trim away any excess fat and skin around the halves. Rinse the meat and pat dry with paper towels.

2   Starting with your chicken bone side up, rub a little olive oil all over the bottom of the chicken, and season well with the ArnieTex Poultry Seasoning Blend. Allow the seasoning to set for 5 minutes, then flip the chicken halves skin side up and repeat this step. Place in the refrigerator for 30 minutes to allow the seasoning to set.

3   With one full, lit chimney of charcoal, set a kettle-style grill's fire cooking temperature for 275°F to 300°F (140°C to 150°C). For added smoke and flavor, add the wood chunks or chips (if using) to the coals, ensuring they are emitting a thin blue or translucent smoke.

4   Place the chickens on the grill, bone side down, directly over the coals. Cover the grill and cook for 1 hour. As long the temperature holds steady, there's no need to open the lid for the first 30 minutes.

5   At the 1-hour mark, check for doneness with a meat thermometer. Probe from the front of the chicken breast; the chicken should be 165°F (75°C) at the thickest part. If it's not, put the lid back on and continue to cook, checking again every 10 to 15 minutes until it's done. This cook usually takes 45 to 60 minutes.

6   For added flavor, you can flip the chicken skin side down during the last 15 minutes to crisp the skin. This adds great texture and flavor to a juicy bite.

7   Remove the chicken from the grill, wrap loosely in foil, and let rest for 10 minutes.

8   Slice or carve to your preference, and serve.

# BEEF RIBS
## [FINGER RIBS]

If you love a tender bite of rib eye and gnawing on rib bones, then you'll love these finger ribs. Also known as back ribs or center-cut ribs, these come next to the rib eye loin, which is why they're so good. The marbling makes for a succulent, juicy bite between the bones and plenty of room for nibbling on them until the last bite.

2 racks of beef back ribs

½ cup ArnieTex Beef Seasoning Blend (page 25)

¼ cup apple cider vinegar

1   Rinse the ribs thoroughly, and completely pat dry with paper towels. Season both sides generously with the ArnieTex Beef Seasoning Blend. Set aside.

2   With one full, lit chimney of charcoal, arrange the grill's fire for dual-zone cooking and set the cooking temperature for 275°F (140°C).

3   Add the ribs to the grill, meat side up, over the indirect heat. Cover the grill, and cook for 30 minutes.

4   Combine ¾ cup of water and the apple cider vinegar in a spray bottle. Evenly spritz the ribs with just enough liquid to moisten the exterior of the meat. Rotate the ribs 180 degrees to help with even cooking. Cover the grill, and cook for 15 more minutes.

5   Uncover the grill, and flip the ribs, meat side down, over the coals. Cook for 1 to 3 minutes to achieve some char, color, and flavor, being careful not to burn the meat.

6   Remove the ribs from the grill. Set them on a piece of foil, meat side down, wrap loosely in the foil, and allow to rest for 10 to 15 minutes. Slice between the bones, and serve.

PREP TIME
15 minutes

COOK TIME
6 hours

SERVES
5 to 6

# BEEF RIBS
## [MONSTER RIBS]

Monster ribs are one of the showstoppers in Texas barbecue. These beef ribs have many names. A butcher shop might have them listed as "plate ribs," "123A ribs," or "English ribs," and they are also nicknamed "dino ribs" or even "brisket on a stick" due to their massive size and similar flavor. Yet these are perhaps even more rich in flavor than the fatty slices of a brisket. When cooked to perfection, monster ribs are super soft, juicy, and melt in your mouth. Similar to a brisket, cooking these correctly requires patience and consistent heat, but when you make it to the end of the cook, the flavor rewards are like no other.

1 rack of beef plate ribs

2 tbsp Worcestershire sauce

3 tbsp ArnieTex Beef Seasoning Blend (page 25)

Wood chunks or chips (your preferred wood; optional)

¼ cup apple cider vinegar

1   Trim off any excessive fat and tough membrane from the meat side of the ribs to help the seasoning blend season the meat directly. Do not remove the membrane from the bone side of the ribs; it will help retain the moisture in the meat during the long cooking process.

2   Thirty minutes before the planned cook time, slather the Worcestershire sauce all over the meat and then evenly season with the ArnieTex Beef Seasoning Blend to cover the entire rack and sides.

3   With one full, lit chimney of charcoal, arrange the grill's fire for dual-zone cooking and set the cooking temperature for 250°F to 275°F (120°C to 140°C). For added smoke and flavor, add the wood chunks (if using) to the coals, ensuring they are emitting a thin blue or translucent smoke.

4   Add the ribs to the grill over indirect heat, with the thickest part of the ribs facing the heat source. Close the grill, and cook for 1 hour.

5   At the 1-hour mark, combine ¾ cup of water and the vinegar in a spray bottle. Spritz the beef ribs. Close the lid and cook for 2 more hours, spritzing at the 2-hour mark and again at the 3-hour mark.

6   After the third spritz, rotate the ribs 180 degrees to encourage even cooking. Cook for 1 more hour.

7   At the 4-hour mark, remove the ribs from the cooker and wrap tightly in foil with the meat side facing down. Return the ribs to the grill and cook for 1 more hour.

8   At the 5-hour mark, check the internal temperature with a meat thermometer. The ribs should be 200°F to 203°F (95°C to 96°C), and the meat should be probe-tender. If the ribs have not yet hit 200°F to 203°F (95°C to 96°C), cook for 30 minutes to 1 hour and then check temperature again.

9   When the ribs hit 200°F to 203°F (95°C to 96°C), remove them from the grill. Place them in a turned-off oven or a cooler for 30 minutes before slicing and serving.

# BEEF RIBS
## [LOADED RIBS]

Loaded beef ribs, also called plate ribs, come from the 123A ribs, which are cut across the bones into ½ to 1-inch (1.25 to 2.5cm) thickness. What you are left with are ribs loaded with marble-rich meat which allows for a juicy bite. (Also see Beef Ribs–Monster Ribs [page 198].)

★ ★ ★

| | | |
|---|---|---|
| 7 lb (3.25kg) loaded beef ribs | ½ cup ArnieTex Beef Seasoning Blend (page 25) | Wood chunks or chips (your preferred wood; optional) |

1 Rinse the ribs thoroughly, and completely pat dry with paper towels. Season both sides of the ribs moderately with the ArnieTex Beef Seasoning Blend. Set aside.

2 With one full, lit chimney of charcoal, arrange the grill's fire for dual-zone cooking and set the cooking temperature for 250°F to 275°F (120°C to 140°C). For added smoke and flavor, add the wood chunks (if using) to the coals, ensuring they are emitting a thin blue or translucent smoke.

3 Add the ribs to the grill over direct heat, placing them so each face the same direction toward the heat. Cover the grill, cook for 10 minutes, and then uncover and flip each of the ribs. Repeat covering, cooking for 10 minutes, and flipping two or three more times until the meat starts to recede into bones and the bones start to slightly pull out from the meat.

4 At the 30- or 40-minute mark, wrap the ribs tightly in foil and place them over indirect heat. Cover the grill and maintain the heat at 250°F to 275°F (120°C to 140°C) for 30 more minutes. Check for doneness with a meat thermometer; the ribs should be 195°F to 200°F (90°C to 95°C) in the thickest part. At this point, the fat and collagen should be fully rendered.

5 Remove from the grill, and allow to rest for 10 minutes. Slice between the bones, and serve.

**8**

# LOS SIDES

# CHARRO BEANS

**PREP TIME**
20 minutes

**COOK TIME**
4 hours

**SERVES**
24

Charro beans, or frijoles charros, draws its name from the Mexican horsemen known as charros. Each version of this dish is as unique and authentic as the family whose recipe has been handed down for generations. One thing common among all the recipes, though, is the use of both pork and vegetables to make a delicious bowl of goodness.

2 lb (1kg) dried pinto beans, picked over and rinsed well

4 strips smoked bacon, diced

3 oz (85g) salt pork, diced

1 hot dog, sliced

6 oz (170g) pork chorizo

½ medium white onion, diced

3 garlic cloves, minced

1 Roma tomato, diced

¼ cup tomato sauce

1 tbsp tomato paste

½ cup chopped fresh cilantro

2 tsp salt

1 tbsp black pepper

2 whole pickled jalapeños

¼ cup fresh cilantro leaves

1 Add the beans to a large heavy-bottomed saucepan, and add 16 cups of water. Set over medium-low heat, bring to a simmer, and cook for 1½ hours.

2 At about the 1-hour mark, heat a 12-inch (30.5cm) skillet over medium-high heat, add the bacon and salt pork, and sauté for 5 minutes. (The rendered fat will provide adequate oil for cooking the rest of the ingredients.)

3 Add the hot dog and chorizo. Break up the chorizo, and cook, stirring, for 5 minutes.

4 Add the onion, and sauté for 5 minutes.

5 Add the garlic, and cook, stirring frequently, for 1 minute.

6 Add the tomato, tomato sauce, and tomato paste, and stir frequently for 2 minutes. Finally, add the chopped cilantro, and stir. Set aside.

7 At the 90-minute mark, add the cooked meats and vegetables to the beans, along with the salt, pepper, and jalapeños.

8 Simmer for 2 more hours, bringing the total cook time to 3½ hours. Taste at this point. If the beans are not fully tender, simmer for another 30 minutes to 1 hour until they are fully soft.

9 Turn off the heat, and stir in the cilantro leaves. Cover, and let rest for 20 minutes before serving.

## COOKING NOTES

*To "pick over" the beans, spread them on a large baking sheet and sort through them, removing any dirt, stones, or bad-looking beans that might be included.*

*Serve these beans on the side of Tacos de Bistec (page 103) with some Papa Asada (page 214).*

# BASIC BEANS
## [TRADITIONAL]

When it comes to refried beans, chalupas, tacos, and sides for my favorite plates, this recipe is my go-to for the beans. These also are my favorite to eat fresh out of the slow cooker en bola (still whole). Finish these beans with a dusting of chile piquín powder or a dab of butter, and you'll see that they're anything but basic.

★ ★ ★

2 cups (14 oz/397g) dried pinto beans, picked over and rinsed well

4 oz (115g) salt pork, diced small

2 strips thick-cut bacon, cut into ½-inch (1.25cm) pieces

2 garlic cloves

3 tsp salt

1 tsp black pepper

1 Add the beans to a 7-quart (6.5-liter) slow cooker along with 8 cups of water. The water should cover the beans by about 1 inch (2.5 cm). Set the slow cooker to high.

2 Add the salt pork, bacon, garlic, salt, and pepper to the beans, and stir. Cover the slow cooker, and let cook for 1 hour.

3 At the 1-hour mark, uncover and stir. Cover again, and cook for 1 more hour.

4 Check at the 2-hour mark. The beans should be fully plump at this point, and the water should still be above the beans. If not, add more water to cover. Cover and cook for 1 more hour.

5 At the 3-hour mark, check for bean tenderness. Taste and adjust the salt if needed. If the beans aren't fully cooked, cook for 1 more hour.

6 Turn off the heat, and let cool for 10 minutes before serving.

## PRO TIPS

*Different brands of pinto beans have some variation in color, flavor, and cook times.*

# REFRIED BEANS
## [THREE WAYS]

These refried beans start with precooked pinto beans from the Charro Beans (page 202) or Basic Beans (Traditional) (page 204) recipes, and I give you three "stages" for different bean textures. Stage 1 beans are great for breakfast plates. Stage 2 is how most restaurants serve beans; they're perfect for every plate of Mexican food and great as a first layer on tortillas for tacos. Stage 3 beans are the ultimate refried beans and my favorite for tostadas or standalone bean and cheese tacos.

2 tbsp lard, bacon grease, or butter, or as needed for your preferred stage

2 cups cooked pinto beans from Charro Beans (page 202) or Basic Beans—Traditional (page 204)

¼ cup chicken broth or water

⅛ tsp salt

⅛ tsp finely ground black pepper (optional)

1   Heat a 10-inch (25.5cm) skillet over medium-high heat. Add the beans, chicken broth, salt, and pepper (if using) to the pan.

2   **For stage 1:** When the beans start to simmer, smash the beans thoroughly and cook for 1 to 3 more minutes. They should be slightly runny, almost a soupy texture and should run smoothly off a spoon. Remove from the heat, and serve immediately.

3   **For stage 2:** Continuing from stage 1's smashing and heating, add 1 tablespoon of lard. Continue stirring and cooking down the beans while evaporating most of the moisture, 1 to 3 more minutes. When the beans start to stick to the bottom of the pan as you stir, they're ready. Remove from the heat, and serve immediately.

4   **For stage 3:** Continuing from stage 2's stirring and cooking, increase the heat to medium-high. Add 1 more tablespoon of lard to the pan. When it melts, stir to incorporate it into the beans. Cook, stirring, until the moisture is completely evaporated and the beans begin to stick together, 1 to 3 more minutes. The beans should be sliding freely around the pan with a slightly crispy and dry texture. Remove from the heat, and serve immediately.

PREP TIME
5 minutes

COOK TIME
35 minutes

SERVES
6 to 8

# MOMMATEX'S MEXICAN RICE

This Mexican rice recipe has been handed down for four generations in my family, and I am honored to share it with you. This rice has color, flavor, texture, and tradition, all in one delicious pan. Serve it as a side with your favorite main dish or alongside Charro Beans (page 202) for a meal. Loved by all who have tasted it, I present my mom's recipe for Mexican rice. Enjoy!

½ tsp salt

1 tsp garlic powder

1 tsp onion powder

1 dash of dried Mexican oregano

½ tsp ground cumin

1 tbsp chicken bouillon

1 tbsp cooking oil

1 cup long-grain white rice

⅓ cup tomato sauce

2 cups warm unsalted chicken broth or water

1 Combine the salt, garlic powder, onion powder, oregano, cumin, and chicken bouillon in a small bowl. Set aside.

2 Heat a 10-inch (25.5cm) skillet over medium-high heat, and add the oil. When the oil is hot, add the rice. Cook, stirring frequently, to develop a slight, toasty tan color on the rice, 10 to 15 minutes.

3 Add the spices to the rice, and stir frequently for 10 to 15 seconds.

4 Add the tomato sauce, stir, and slowly add the warm chicken broth or water. Stir a bit more as the pan comes to a medium simmer. Cover, reduce the heat to low, and simmer for 15 minutes.

5 Remove from the heat, and allow to rest, covered, for 5 minutes.

6 Remove the lid, fluff with a fork, and serve.

# GUACAMOLE

Guacamole is a universal dish with an infinite number of subtleties depending on the recipe. Mine is simple, adding only a scoop of Pico de Gallo (page 34) to the perfectly ripe avocados and mashing to a perfect consistency. This simple addition allows the avocados to take center stage in this recipe. Serve with your favorite tortilla chips, or use to top a number of dishes for a boost of flavor.

★ ★ ★

3 medium ripe avocados, peeled and pitted

1 Roma tomato, diced

¼ medium white onion, diced

1 clove garlic, minced

1 jalapeño or serrano chile, diced

20 cilantro leaves, coarsely chopped

Juice of 1 lime

2 tsp salt

1  Add the avocados to a bowl, along with the tomato, onion, garlic, jalapeño or serrano, cilantro, lime juice, and salt. Using a fork, mash the ingredients to a semi-chunky consistency.

2  Serve immediately.

## COOKING NOTES

*You can substitute ½ cup Pico de Gallo (page 34) for the tomato, onion, garlic, jalapeño or serrano, cilantro, and lime juice. Reduce the salt from 2 teaspoons to ½ teaspoon to account for the salt in the Pico de Gallo.*

# QUICK PICKLED ONIONS

**PREP TIME**
10 minutes plus
2 hours 30 minutes
to cool

**COOK TIME**
15 minutes

**MAKES**
2 (16-oz/473ml)
canning jars

A delicious condiment to keep in your refrigerator, these pickled onions add a tangy boost of flavor, especially to a plate of street tacos.

★ ★ ★

2 medium red or white onions, cut in half and then cut into thin half moons

1 serrano chile, cut in half lengthwise

½ tsp black pepper, divided

½ tsp red pepper flakes (optional), divided

1 bay leaf, cut in half

**BRINE**

1 cup white vinegar

½ cup sugar

¼ cup coarse kosher salt

1 Lightly pack 1 onion into each of two 16-ounce (473ml) canning jars. Set aside.

2 Add the brine ingredients to a small saucepan along with 2 cups of water. Set the saucepan over medium-high heat, and bring to a slow boil. Once boiling, turn off the heat.

3 Add half a serrano, ¼ teaspoon black pepper, ¼ teaspoon red pepper flakes (if using), and half a bay leaf to each jar.

4 Fill the jars with the hot brine. Set aside to allow to cool completely, at least 30 minutes, uncovered.

5 Add the lids, tighten them snugly, and place the jars in the refrigerator for at least 2 hours before serving; overnight is better. Keeps in the refrigerator for up to 2 weeks.

# TOTOPOS

**PREP TIME**
5 minutes

**COOK TIME**
10 minutes

**SERVES**
7 to 10

Totopos (tortilla chips) are the quintessential must-have for every salsa, guacamole, refried bean dip, carne asada, and so many other scoopable dishes. There are no store-bought chips nearly as good as homemade totopos—frying them yourself and shaking on some salt or your favorite seasoning while they're still warm. That fresh, warm flavor is unmatched. They also make a great snack with some melted cheese on top.

★ ★ ★

4 cups frying oil        20 corn tortillas        1 pinch of salt

1  Add the oil to a large saucepan, set over medium-high heat, and heat to 350°F (180°C).

2  Stack the tortillas in small piles and cut them down the middle. Rotate the stacks 90 degrees, and cut again for perfect quarters. Repeat for the remaining tortillas.

3  When the oil is hot, add about a quarter of the cut tortillas. You want to see how they land in the oil first and not overcrowd them, especially the first batch.

4  Using tongs or a spider strainer, gently move the tortillas around as they fry to avoid sticking.

5  As soon as the totopos float, they are ready to be removed. If you prefer a slightly more golden-brown finish, you can leave them in for an additional 30 seconds, stirring occasionally.

6  Strain and transfer the totopos to a bowl, season with a pinch of salt, and toss to distribute evenly.

7  Repeat with the tortillas. Serve warm.

## COOKING NOTES

*I prefer to use a 5-quart (4.75-liter) saucepan for this recipe, but you can use your favorite deep-frying pot. The key is to ensure the oil can fully submerge the chips after they're dropped in. If you're using something larger, such as an 8-quart (7.5-liter) stockpot, you'll need to use more oil. It's also helpful to use a cooking thermometer to ensure the oil is (and stays) hot enough. The totopos will soak up too much oil if it's not hot enough.*

# CHORIQUESO

Choriqueso, a combination of chorizo and melted cheese, is one of the most popular appetizers along the South Texas border. It's common in many restaurants, but for my family, it's most iconic when served alongside guacamole as we wait for the grilled cabrito (goat kid) to be served. One bite of this, and you'll be hooked for life!

★ ★ ★

| 24 oz (680g) pork chorizo | 20 oz (560g) grated Oaxaca cheese | 10 corn tortillas, warmed |
|---|---|---|

1  Preheat the oven to 350°F (180°C).

2  Heat a large oven-safe skillet over medium heat. When hot, add the chorizo, and sauté, breaking up any chunks, for 10 minutes. When the chorizo is fully cooked, turn off the heat.

3  Remove ¼ cup of chorizo from the pan and set aside.

4  Completely cover the chorizo in the skillet with the cheese, and put the pan in the oven until the cheese is completely melted and starting to bubble, 3 to 5 minutes.

5  Remove from the oven and let rest for 5 minutes.

6  Garnish the Choriqueso with the reserved chorizo, and serve.

## PRO TIPS

*For flare when serving, drop a warm corn tortilla onto the choriqueso, squeeze to fill the tortilla with choriqueso, and slowly pull away. Now, pause! Take your phone out and be sure to snap a picture of this awesome shot, so that your friends know what they missed out on!*

# PAPA ASADA

**PREP TIME**
5 minutes

**COOK TIME**
1 hour

**SERVES**
2

Papa Asada is a beautiful, and sometimes elusive, side dish at taquerias. In the lower Rio Grande Valley, it isn't too common to find it on the menu, yet travel just a couple counties northward to the upper Rio Grande Valley, and you will find most taquerias have combo meals consisting of an order of tacos, a cup of charro beans, and papa asada smothered in butter, melted cheese, a dollop of sour cream or Mexican crema, and sometimes even bacon! Got a big appetite? Top this recipe with a hearty portion of bistec (see page 103) or Easy Al Pastor (page 92).

1 large russet potato (the bigger the better)

4 tbsp unsalted butter

¼ to ½ cup grated American or cheddar cheese

Pinch of salt

Pinch of black pepper

1–3 tbsp sour cream (optional)

1  Preheat the oven to 350°F (180°C).

2  Rinse the potato well, tightly double wrap in foil, and place on a baking sheet.

3  Bake for at least 45 minutes or up to 1 hour, if needed, until the potato is very soft and squeezable.

4  Remove the potato from the oven and let cool for 5 to 10 minutes.

5  Set the potato on a plate, and unwrap the foil. Slice the potato down the middle, end to end, but not all the way down so it's still one piece.

6  Add the butter, cheese, a pinch of salt and pepper, and sour cream (if using). Mix thoroughly with a fork until you have formed a soft, almost mashed potato–like texture inside the skin.

7  Serve immediately alongside Tacos de Bistec (page 103) or any of the fajitas (pages 107 through 111), or with Totopos (page 211).

## PRO TIPS

*Add 2 or 3 tablespoons of your favorite salsa during step 6 to bring a whole other world of flavor to the papa.*

# POTATO SALAD

**PREP TIME**
20 minutes plus
2 hours to chill

**COOK TIME**
30 minutes

**SERVES**
14

I count myself lucky that I have two of the best potato salad recipes in the world under my roof. Who would have thought that when I introduced Terry (then my girlfriend, now my wife) to MommaTex some 42 years ago, their potato salad recipes would be nearly identical? Needless to say, for all the infinite ways there are to make potato salad, we have found that this is our family favorite. I hope you enjoy it!

| | | |
|---|---|---|
| 2 lb (1kg) russet potatoes | ⅓ cup yellow mustard | ½ cup finely diced celery |
| 3 large eggs | 1 tbsp dill pickle juice | ⅓ cup finely diced dill pickles |
| 1 cup mayonnaise | 1½ tsp salt | A few dashes smoked paprika |

1 Fill an 8-quart (7.5-liter) stockpot two thirds full of water, and set over high heat. Add the potatoes and eggs, and bring to a rolling boil. Remove and set aside the eggs after 15 minutes, and continue boiling the potatoes until they are fork-tender, about 10 to 15 more minutes. Strain the potatoes, and transfer to a large bowl.

2 While the potatoes cool, peel and finely dice the eggs.

3 In a small bowl, thoroughly combine the mayonnaise, mustard, pickle juice, and salt.

4 Peel the potatoes, cut them into ½- to ¾-inch (1.25–2cm) cubes, and return them to the large bowl. Add the eggs, celery, and pickles, and gently stir to incorporate. Pour the dressing over the mixture, and stir gently again to incorporate.

5 Cover the bowl with plastic wrap, and set in the refrigerator for at least 2 hours before serving. Sprinkle with paprika for color before serving.

## PRO TIPS

*Here are the two differences between my wife's recipe and MommaTex's recipe: 2 tablespoons of sliced olives (Terry) and 2 tablespoons of finely diced white onion (MommaTex). A lot of flavor is added with these two ingredients, and I encourage you to try both.*

# ACKNOWLEDGMENTS

I can't express my gratitude enough to my fans, subscribers, and followers, who pushed me to write a cookbook in the first place. You planted that seed in my head years ago and encouraged me to believe it was possible. Now here it is! This fun, crazy online world of ArnieTex would be nothing without your support. Thank you.

And to my family, who have always been here by my side, encouraging me and inspiring me to pursue what I love. Thank you for cheering me up when I needed it and for helping me through an impossible year of challenges and obstacles to get here. We made it!

# INDEX

## A

achiote (annatto), 24
    Al Pastor Adobo, 59
    Red Carnicería Marinade, 60
adobos, 25
Al Pastor Adobo
    Easy al Pastor Tacos, 92
    recipe, 59
American cheese
    Botana (RGV Style), 126
    Crispy Tacos, 94
    Hamburgesa Mexicana, 116
    Migas, 81
    Papa Asada, 214
    Tex-Mex Enchiladas, 150–151
applewood, 23
ancho chiles. *See* chiles ancho
árbol, chiles de. *See* chiles
    de árbol
ArnieTex Beef Seasoning Blend
    Beef Ribs (Finger Ribs), 196
    Beef Ribs (Loaded Ribs), 199
    Beef Ribs (Monster Ribs), 198
    Fajitas—Skirt Steak, 107
    Mollejas, 173
    Parrillada, 164
    recipe, 25
    Steak (Porterhouse or T-Bone),
      119
    Steak (Rib Eye), 121
    Steak Ranchero, 130
ArnieTex Pork Seasoning Blend
    Dove Poppers, 166
    Pork Belly Chicharrón, 188–189
    Pulled Pork, 183
    recipe, 25
    Texas Pork Ribs, 187
ArnieTex Poultry Seasoning Blend
    Chicken Fajitas, 111
    Enchiladas Suizas, 146–147
    Grilled Chicken Thighs, 191
    recipe, 25
    Smoked Turkey Breast, 190
    Texas Chicken Halves, 195
ArnieTex Tejano Burger, 115
Arroz con Pollo, 136
Asado de Puerco, 125
ash scraper, 16, 18
avocado(s)
    Carnitas, 174
    Ceviche, 154
    Crispy Tacos, 94
    Guacamole, 208
    Hamburgesa Mexicana, 116
    Pico de Gallo, 34
    Salsa Verde—Aguacate, 44
    Tacos de Bistec, 103
    Tortas de Deshebrada, 96
avocado oil, 27

## B

bacon
    Basic Beans (Traditional), 204
    Charro Beans, 202
    Con Huevos—Bacon, 70
    Discada Norteña, 159
    Dove Poppers, 166
    Hamburgesa Mexicana, 116
    Sombrero Plate, 129
Baja Fish and Shrimp Tacos, 95
Barbacoa Especial, 73
barbecue competitions, 12, 14
barbecue sauce(s), 26
    Dove Poppers, 166
    Texas Pork Ribs, 187
barbecue spritzes, 26
barbecue tools, 16, *18–19*
Basic Beans (Traditional), 204
    adding to Texas Chili, 161
    Refried Beans (Three Ways),
      205
bay leaves, 24
beans. *See* pinto beans
beef. *See also* chuck; ground beef;
    skirt steaks; steak
    Birria de Res, 170–171
    Cacheteadas, 100
    Carne con Papas, 134
    Carne Guisada, 122–123
    Chile Colorado, 140–141
    common grades of, 31
    dried, in Machacado à la
      Mexicana, 82
    Fajitas—Restaurant Style, 108
    Tacos de Bistec, 103
    Tortas de Deshebrada, 96
beef back ribs, in Beef Ribs (Finger
    Ribs), 196
beef broth
    Birria de Res, 170–171
    Chile Colorado, 140–141
    Smoked Barbacoa, 169
    Texas Chili, 160–161

beef chorizo, in Con Huevos—
    Chorizo, 71
beef fajitas
    Fajitas—Restaurant Style, 108
    Fajitas—Skirt Steak, 107
    Parrillada, 164
beef marrow bones, in Salsa
    Tuétano, 65
Beef Ribs (Finger Ribs), 196
Beef Ribs (Loaded Ribs), 199
Beef Ribs (Monster Ribs), 198
beef seasoning blend. *See*
    ArnieTex Beef Seasoning Blend
beef shank, in Caldo de Res, 153
beef soup bones, in Caldo de Res,
    153
beef tallow, 27
beef tongue
    Barbacoa Especial, 73
    Smoked Barbacoa, 169
beef tripe, in Menudo, 163
beer
    Baja Fish and Shrimp Tacos, 95
    Discada Norteña, 159
bell pepper
    Carne con Papas, 134
    Carne Guisada, 122–123
    Chicken Fajitas, 111
    Discada Norteña, 159
    Dove Poppers, 166
    Fajitas—Restaurant Style, 108
    Fideo, 167
    Picadillo, 144
    Pollo Guisado, 155
    Sombrero Plate, 129
    Texas Chili, 160–161
    Tortas de Deshebrada, 96
Birria de Res, 170–171
black pepper, 24
bolillo breads, in Tortas de
    Deshebrada, 96
Botana (RGV Style), 126
bread (Pan de Campo), 177
brisket, 14, 28
    Texas Brisket, 184–185
Brisket Masterclass, 14
burgers
    ArnieTex Tejano Burger, 115
    Hamburgesa Mexicana, 116
butchers, 28, 31

# C

cabbage
    Baja Fish and Shrimp Tacos, 95
    Caldo de Res, 153
cachete (beef cheek meat), in
    Smoked Barbacoa, 169
Calabaza con Pollo, 139
calabaza squash
    Calabaza con Pollo, 139
    Caldo de Pollo, 135
    Caldo de Res, 153
Caldo de Pollo, 135
Caldo de Res, 153
canola oil, 27
Carne con Papas, 134
Carne Guisada, 122–123
Carnitas, 174
carrot(s)
    Caldo de Pollo, 135
    Caldo de Res, 153
    Picadillo, 144
    Texas Chili, 160–161
    Tortas de Deshebrada, 96
celery
    Caldo de Pollo, 135
    Caldo de Res, 153
    Carne Guisada, 122–123
    Potato Salad, 215
    Texas Chili, 160–161
    Tortas de Deshebrada, 96
Ceviche, 154
chalpuas, 133
charcoal briquettes, 22, 23
charcoal chimneys, 22
Charro Beans
    recipe, 202
    Refried Beans (Three Ways),
       205
cheddar cheese
    ArnieTex Tejano Burger, 115
    Costra de Queso, 89
    Papa Asada, 214
    Texas Chili Enchiladas, 149
    Tex-Mex Enchiladas, 150–151
    Tostadas (aka Chalupas), 133
cheek meat
    Barbacoa Especial, 73
    Smoked Barbacoa, 169
cheese. See American cheese;
    cheddar cheese; Oaxaca
    cheese; queso fresco
chicharrón con carnita, in
    Chicharrón en Salsa Verde, 77
chicken. See also whole chicken
    Arroz con Pollo, 136
    Calabaza con Pollo, 139
    Caldo de Pollo, 135
    Chicken Fajitas, 111
    Enchiladas Suizas, 146–147

Flautas, 143
    Grilled Chicken Leg Quarters,
       192
    Grilled Chicken Thighs, 191
    Pollo Guisado, 155
chicken broth
    Arroz con Pollo, 136
    Asado de Puerco, 125
    Calabaza con Pollo, 139
    Carne con Papas, 134
    Chile Colorado, 140–141
    Fideo, 167
    Flautas, 143
    Mommatex's Mexican Rice,
       207
    Picadillo, 144
    Pollo Guisado, 155
    Refried Beans (Three Ways),
       205
chicken fajitas
    Chicken Fajitas, 111
    Parrillada, 164
Chilaquiles Rojos, 78
Chile Colorado, 140–141
Chile Guajillo Sauce, 56
    Enchiladas Rojas, 145
    Menudo, 163
    Tamales, 178–179
chiles ancho, 26
    Al Pastor Adobo, 59
    Asado de Puerco, 125
    Birria de Res, 170–171
    Chile Guajillo Sauce, 56
    Salsa Macha, 55
chiles de árbol
    about, 26
    Al Pastor Adobo, 59
    Asado de Puerco, 125
    Birria de Res, 170–171
    Chilaquiles Rojos, 78
    Chile Guajillo Sauce, 56
    Fire-Roasted Salsa, 48
    Salsa Macha, 55
    Salsa Puya, 52
    Salsa Roja—Taqueria, 39
    Salsa Taquera, 45
    Salsa Tatemada, 64
    Salsa Verde—Tomatillos, 42
    Tortas de Deshebrada, 96
chiles, dried, 26–27
chiles guajillo, 27
    Al Pastor Adobo, 59
    Asado de Puerco, 125
    Birria de Res, 170–171
    Chilaquiles Rojos, 78
    Chile Colorado, 140–141
    Chile Guajillo Sauce, 56
    Salsa Macha, 55
    Salsa Puya, 52
    Salsa Tatemada, 64
    Tortas de Deshebrada, 96

chiles pasillas, 27
    Birria de Res, 170–171
chiles piquín, in Salsa Chile Piquín,
    51
chile poblano
    Enchiladas Suizas, 146–147
    Tacos Gobernador, 99
chiles puya
    Chilaquiles Rojos, 78
    Salsa Puya, 52
Chile Toreados
    recipe, 63
    Sombrero Plate, 129
chili (canned), in Texas Chili
    Enchiladas, 149
chili peppers. See jalapeños;
    serrano chiles
Chili, Texas, 160–161
chipotles, 26
chipotles in adobo sauce
    Al Pastor Adobo, 59
    Baja Fish and Shrimp Tacos, 95
    Salsa Chipotle en Adobo, 50
choice-grade beef, 31
Choripapas, 74
Choriqueso, 213
chorizo
    Charro Beans, 202
    Choripapas, 74
    Choriqueso, 213
    Con Huevos—Chorizo, 71
    Discada Norteña, 159
chuck
    Birria de Res, 170–171
    Carne con Papas, 134
    Carne Guisada, 122–123
    Chile Colorado, 140–141
    Tacos de Bistec, 103
    Tortas de Deshebrada, 96
cilantro, 24
    Barbacoa Especial, 73
    Birria de Res, 170–171
    Cacheteadas, 100
    Caldo de Pollo, 135
    Caldo de Res, 153
    Carnitas, 174
    Charro Beans, 202
    Con Huevos—Nopales, 72
    Discada Norteña, 159
    Easy al Pastor Tacos, 92
    Enchiladas Suizas, 146–147
    Fajitas—Restaurant Style, 108
    Fideo, 167
    Flautas, 143
    Green Fajita Marinade, 62
    Gringas, 93
    Guacamole, 208
    Mollejas, 173
    Picadillo, 144
    Pico de Gallo, 34
    Salsa Chipotle en Adobo, 50

Salsa Roja—Boiled, 38
Salsa Tuétano, 65
Salsa Verde—Aguacate, 44
Salsa Verde—Tomatillos, 42
Smoked Barbacoa, 169
Sombrero Plate, 129
Steak Ranchero, 130
Tacos de Bistec, 103
Tacos Gobernador, 99
cinnamon, 24
cinnamon stick
    Al Pastor Adobo, 59
    Birria de Res, 170–171
clove, 24
coarse kosher salt, 25
cola, in Carnitas, 174
Con Huevos—Bacon, 70
Con Huevos—Chorizo, 71
Con Huevos—Nopales, 72
Con Huevos—Papas, 68
consommés/bouillons, 26
corn (ears)
    Calabaza con Pollo, 139
    Caldo de Pollo, 135
    Caldo de Res, 153
corn (frozen), in Picadillo, 144
corn tortillas
    Baja Fish and Shrimp Tacos, 95
    Barbacoa Especial, 73
    Cacheteadas, 100
    Carnitas, 174
    Chilaquiles Rojos, 78
    Choriqueso, 213
    Con Huevos—Nopales, 72
    Crispy Tacos, 94
    Easy al Pastor Tacos, 92
    Enchiladas Rojas, 145
    Enchiladas Suizas, 146–147
    Fajitas—Restaurant Style, 108
    Fajitas—Skirt Steak, 107
    Flautas, 143
    Menudo, 163
    Migas, 81
    Mollejas, 173
    Sombrero Plate, 129
    Tacos de Bistec, 103
    Tacos Gobernador, 99
    Texas Chili Enchiladas, 149
    Tex-Mex Enchiladas, 150–151
    Tostadas (aka Chalupas), 133
    Totopos, 211
Costra de Queso, 89
cowboy bread (Pan de Campo), 177
cream cheese
    Dove Poppers, 166
    Enchiladas Suizas, 146–147
Creamy Habanero Salsa, 47
Crispy Tacos, 94
cumin, 24

## D

Diamond kosher salt, 25
dill pickle juice
    Hamburgesa Mexicana, 116
    Potato Salad, 215
dill pickles
    ArnieTex Tejano Burger, 115
    Potato Salad, 215
Discada Norteña, 159
dove breasts, in Dove Poppers, 166

## E

Easy al Pastor Tacos
    Gringas, 93
    recipe, 92
eggs
    Con Huevos—Bacon, 70
    Con Huevos—Chorizo, 71
    Con Huevos—Nopales, 72
    Con Huevos—Papas, 68
    Huevos Divorciados, 86
    Huevos Rancheros, 85
    Machacado à la Mexicana, 82
    Migas, 81
    Potato Salad, 215
elevation, cook times and, 31
enchiladas
    Enchiladas Rojas, 145
    Enchiladas Suizas, 146–147
    Texas Chili Enchiladas, 149
    Tex-Mex Enchiladas, 150–151
Enchilada Sauce, 150–151

## F

fajitas
    Botana (RGV Style), 126
    Chicken Fajitas, 111
    Discada Norteña, 159
    Fajitas—Restaurant Style, 108
    Fajitas—Skirt Steak, 107
    Parrillada, 164
    Sombrero Plate, 129
Fideo, 167
Finger Ribs, 196
fire control, 31
Fire-Roasted Salsa, 48
fire starters, 22
fish and seafood
    Baja Fish and Shrimp Tacos, 95
    Ceviche, 154
    Tacos Gobernador, 99
flap meat
    Fajitas—Restaurant Style, 108
    Steak Ranchero, 130

Flautas, 143
flour tortillas
    Barbacoa Especial, 73
    Chicken Fajitas, 111
    Con Huevos—Chorizo, 71
    Fajitas—Restaurant Style, 108
    Fajitas—Skirt Steak, 107
    Gringas, 93
fuel, types of, 23

## G

garlic, 27
ghee, 27
gloves, 16, *18*
Green Fajita Marinade, 62
green peas, in Picadillo, 144
Grilled Chicken Leg Quarters, 192
Grilled Chicken Thighs, 191
grills, 20–21
Gringas, 93
ground beef
    ArnieTex Tejano Burger, 115
    Crispy Tacos, 94
    Hamburgesa Mexicana, 116
    Picadillo, 144
    Texas Chili, 160–161
    Tex-Mex Enchiladas, 150–151
Guacamole
    Botana (RGV Style), 126
    Fajitas—Restaurant Style, 108
    Fajitas—Skirt Steak, 107
    recipe, 208
guajillo chiles. *See* chiles guajillo

## H

habanero peppers, 26
Habanero Salsa, Creamy, 47
halibut
    Baja Fish and Shrimp, 95
    Ceviche, 154
ham
    Discada Norteña, 159
    Hamburgesa Mexicana, 116
    Tortas de Deshebrada, 96
hamburger buns
    ArnieTex Tejano Burger, 115
    Hamburgesa Mexicana, 116
hardwood logs, *22, 23*
herbs, 24
hickory wood, 23
hominy, in Menudo, 163
hot dog, in Charro Beans, 202
Huevos Divorciados, 86
Huevos Rancheros, 85

# I

iceberg lettuce
    ArnieTex Tejano Burger, 115
    Crispy Tacos, 94
    Enchiladas Rojas, 145
    Flautas, 143
    Hamburgesa Mexicana, 116
    Tortas de Deshebrada, 96
    Tostadas (aka Chalupas), 133
International Barbeque Cookers
    Association Hall of Fame, 14

# J

jalapeños, 26. *See also* pickled
    jalapeños
    Caldo de Pollo, 135
    Chile Toreados, 63
    Discada Norteña, 159
    Dove Poppers, 166
    Enchiladas Suizas, 146–147
    Fire-Roasted Salsa, 48
    Green Fajita Marinade, 62
    Guacamole, 208
    Hamburgesa Mexicana, 116
    Machacado à la Mexicana, 82
    Parrillada, 164
    Picadillo, 144
    Pico de Gallo, 34
    Salsa Roja—Taqueria, 39
    Salsa Tatemada, 64
    Salsa Verde—Aguacate, 44
    Salsa Verde—Base, 40
    Salsa Verde—Taqueria, 43
    Salsa Verde—Tomatillos, 42
    Sombrero Plate, 129
    Steak Ranchero, 130
    Tortas de Deshebrada, 96

# K

kettles, 20, *21*
kitchen tools, 17, 19
knives, 16, *18*
Kobe cows, 31
kosher salt, 25

# L

la mano (a pinch of this and that),
    28
lard, 27

lemon
    Ceviche, 154
    Con Huevos—Nopales, 72
    Green Fajita Marinade, 62
    Pico de Gallo, 34
lengua (beef tongue). *See* beef
    tongue
lighter fluid, 22
lime
    Birria de Res, 170–171
    Caldo de Pollo, 135
    Caldo de Res, 153
    Ceviche, 154
    Con Huevos—Nopales, 72
    Discada Norteña, 159
    Easy al Pastor Tacos, 92
    Enchiladas Rojas, 145
    Green Fajita Marinade, 62
    Guacamole, 208
    Hamburgesa Mexicana, 116
    Mollejas, 173
    Pico de Gallo, 34
    Red Carnicería Marinade, 60
    Salsa Tatemada, 64
    Salsa Tuétano, 65
    Tacos Gobernador, 99
    Tostadas (aka Chalupas), 133
Loaded Ribs, 199
long lighters, 22, *22*
lump charcoal, 22, 23

# M

machaca, in Machacado à la
    Mexicana, 82
"make it work" mantra, 28
marinades, 26
    Al Pastor Adobo, 59
    Green Fajita Marinade, 62
    Red Carnicería Marinade, 60
masa harina, in Tamales, 178–179
meat grinder, 17
meat, resting, 31
Menudo, 163
mesquite wood, 23
Mexican cinnamon, 24
Mexican crema
    Baja Fish and Shrimp Tacos, 95
    Enchiladas Suizas, 146–147
    Flautas, 143
    Hamburgesa Mexicana, 116
    Tortas de Deshebrada, 96
Migas, 81
Mirepoix, in Texas Chili, 160–161
molcajete, 17
Mollejas (sweetbreads), 173
MommaTex's Mexican Rice
    Botana (RGV Style), 126
    Caldo de Pollo, 135
    Caldo de Res, 153

    Fajitas—Restaurant Style, 108
    recipe, 207
Monster Ribs, 198
Monterey Jack cheese, in
    Enchiladas Suizas, 146–147

# N

natural wood splits, *22, 23*
noodles, in Fideo, 167
nopales, in Con Huevos—Nopales,
    72

# O

Oaxaca cheese
    Choriqueso, 213
    Costra de Queso, 89
    Enchiladas Suizas, 146–147
    Gringas, 93
    Sombrero Plate, 129
    Tacos Gobernador, 99
    Tortas de Deshebrada, 96
oils, types of, 27
olive oil, extra-virgin, 27
onions, 27
Onions, Quick Pickled, 210
open-fire grills, 20, *21*
orange/orange juice
    Carnitas, 174
    Green Fajita Marinade, 62
    Red Carnicería Marinade, 60
oregano, 24
outdoor griddles, 21, *21*

# P

packer brisket, in Texas Brisket,
    184–185
Pan de Campo (cowboy bread), 177
Papa Asada, 214
paprika, 24
Parrillada, 164
parsley, in Green Fajita Marinade,
    62
pasillas chiles. *See* chiles pasillas
peanuts, in Salsa Macha, 55
pear burners, 22, *22*
pecan wood, 23
pellet grills and smokers, 20, *21*
pellets, *22, 23*
Picadillo, 144
pickled jalapeños
    Botana (RGV Style), 126
    Charro Beans, 202

Pickled Onions, Quick, 210
pickle juice. *See* dill pickle juice
pickles. *See* dill pickles
Pico de Gallo
    Barbacoa Especial with, 73
    Ceviche, 154
    Fajitas—Skirt Steak, 107
    Mollejas, 173
    recipe, 34
pineapple/pineapple juice
    Al Pastor Adobo, 59
    Easy al Pastor Tacos, 92
    Green Fajita Marinade, 62
    Gringas, 93
    Red Carnicería Marinade, 60
pinto beans. *See also* Refried
    Beans (Three Ways)
    Basic Beans (Traditional), 204
    Charro Beans, 202
Pitmaster Class, 14
plate ribs
    Beef Ribs (Loaded Ribs), 199
    Beef Ribs (Monster Ribs), 198
poblano chile. *See* chile poblano
Pollo Guisado, 155
pork. *See also* bacon; ham
    Carnitas, 174
    Discada Norteña, 159
    Easy al Pastor Tacos, 92
    Pork Belly Chicharrón, 188–189
    Texas Pork Ribs, 187
Pork Belly Chicharrón, 188–189
pork butt
    Asado de Puerco, 125
    Carnitas, 174
    Pulled Pork, 183
    Tamales, 178–179
pork chops, in Cacheteadas, 100
pork chorizo
    Charro Beans, 202
    Choriqueso, 213
    Con Huevos—Chorizo, 71
pork feet, in Menudo, 163
pork lard
    Carnitas, 174
    Easy al Pastor Tacos, 92
pork roast, in Easy al Pastor Tacos,
    92
pork seasoning blend. *See*
    ArnieTex Pork Seasoning Blend
portable grills, 20, *21*
Porterhouse Steak, 119
post oak wood, 23
potatoes
    Caldo de Pollo, 135
    Caldo de Res, 153
    Carne con Papas, 134
    Choripapas, 74
    Con Huevos—Papas, 68
    Huevos Divorciados, 86
    Papa Asada, 214

Picadillo, 144
    Potato Salad, 215
Potato Salad, 215
poultry seasoning blend. *See*
    ArnieTex Poultry Seasoning
    Blend
prime beef, 31
pro tips, 28–31
Pulled Pork, 183
puya chiles. *See* chiles puya

## Q

queso Chihuahua, in Enchiladas
    Suizas, 146–147
queso fresco
    Enchiladas Rojas, 145
    Flautas, 143
    Tostadas (aka Chalupas), 133
queso Oaxaca, in Enchiladas
    Suizas, 146–147
Quick Pickled Onions, 210

## R

Red Carnicería Marinade, 60
red snapper, in Ceviche, 154
Refried Beans (Three Ways)
    Botana (RGV Style), 126
    Fajitas—Restaurant Style, 108
    Huevos Divorciados, 86
    recipe, 205
    Tortas de Deshebrada, 96
    Tostadas (aka Chalupas), 133
resting meat, 31
rib eye
    Cacheteadas, 100
    Steak (Rib Eye), 121
ribs
    Beef Ribs (Finger Ribs), 196
    Beef Ribs (Loaded Ribs), 199
    Beef Ribs (Monster Ribs), 198
    Texas Pork Ribs, 187
rice, in Arroz con Pollo, 136. *See also*
    MommaTex's Mexican Rice
Roma tomatoes
    Birria de Res, 170–171
    Botana (RGV Style), 126
    Calabaza con Pollo, 139
    Caldo de Res, 153
    Carne con Papas, 134
    Carne Guisada, 122–123
    Charro Beans, 202
    Chilaquiles Rojos, 78
    Chile Colorado, 140–141
    Con Huevos—Nopales, 72
    Crispy Tacos, 94
    Discada Norteña, 159

Enchiladas Rojas, 145
Fideo, 167
Fire-Roasted Salsa, 48
Flautas, 143
Guacamole, 208
Hamburgesa Mexicana, 116
Machacado à la Mexicana, 82
Picadillo, 144
Pico de Gallo, 34
Pollo Guisado, 155
Salsa Chile Piquín, 51
Salsa Chipotle en Adobo, 50
Salsa Roja—Boiled, 38
Salsa Roja—Ranchera, 37
Salsa Roja—Taqueria, 39
Salsa Taquera, 45
Salsa Tatemada, 64
Salsa Tuétano, 65
Sombrero Plate, 129
Steak Ranchero, 130
Tacos Gobernador, 99
Texas Chili, 160–161
Tortas de Deshebrada, 96
Tostadas (aka Chalupas), 133

## S

Salsa Chile Piquín, 51
Salsa Chipotle en Adobo, 50
Salsa Macha, 55
Salsa Puya, 52
salsa recipes
    Creamy Habanero Salsa, 47
    Fire-Roasted Salsa, 48
    Pico de Gallo, 34
    Salsa Chipotle en Adobo, 50
    Salsa Macha, 55
    Salsa Puya, 52
    Salsa Roja—Boiled, 38
    Salsa Roja—Ranchera, 37
    Salsa Roja—Taqueria, 39
    Salsa Taquera, 45
    Salsa Tatemada, 64
    Salsa Verde—Aguacate, 44
    Salsa Verde—Base, 40
    Salsa Verde—Taqueria, 43
    Salsa Verde—Tomatillos, 42
Salsa Roja—Boiled, 38
Salsa Roja—Ranchera, 37
    Huevos Divorciados, 86
    Huevos Rancheros, 85
Salsa Roja—Taqueria, 39
    Tacos de Bistec, 103
Salsa Taquera
    recipe, 45
    Sombrero Plate, 129
Salsa Tatemada, 64
Salsa Tuétano, 65
Salsa Verde—Aguacate, 44
Salsa Verde—Base, 40

Salsa Verde—Taqueria
    recipe, 43
    Tacos de Bistec, 103
Salsa Verde—Tomatillos, 42
    Cacheteadas, 100
    Chicharrón en Salsa Verde, 77
    Huevos Divorciados, 86
salt, 24–25, 31
salt pork
    Basic Beans (Traditional), 204
    Charro Beans, 202
sandwiches
    Pulled Pork, 183
    Tortas de Deshebrada, 96
Santa Maria grills, 20, 21
saucepans, 16, 18
sausage, in Parrillada, 164. See also
    chorizo
sea salt, 25
seasonings, 24–25
select-grade beef, 31
serrano chiles, 26
    Chile Toreados, 63
    Discada Norteña, 159
    Guacamole, 208
    Pico de Gallo, 34
    Quick Pickled Onions, 210
    Salsa Chipotle en Adobo, 50
    Salsa Roja—Boiled, 38
    Salsa Roja—Ranchera, 37
    Salsa Taquera, 45
    Salsa Tuétano, 65
    Salsa Verde—Base, 40
    Salsa Verde—Tomatillos, 42
    Sombrero Plate, 129
sesame seeds, in Salsa Macha, 55
shrimp
    Baja Fish and Shrimp Tacos, 95
    Ceviche, 154
    Tacos Gobernador, 99
skirt steaks
    Cacheteadas, 100
    Discada Norteña, 159
    Fajitas—Skirt Steak, 107
    Sombrero Plate, 129
slaw, in Baja Fish and Shrimp
    Tacos, 95
smoke, 26
Smoked Barbacoa, 169
Smoked Turkey Breast, 190
smokers, 20, 21
Sombrero Plate, 129
soups
    Caldo de Res, 153
    Menudo, 163
spices, 24
spinning asado crosses, 20–21, 21
spritzes, barbecue, 26
squash. See calabaza squash

steak. See also chuck; skirt steaks
    Porterhouse Steak, 119
    Rib Eye Steak, 121
    Steak Ranchero, 130
    T-Bone Steak, 119
Steak (Porterhouse or T-Bone), 119
Steak Ranchero, 130
stews
    Asado de Puerco, 125
    Pollo Guisado, 155

## T-U-V

table salt, 25
tablitas, in Parrillada, 164
tacos
    Baja Fish and Shrimp Tacos, 95
    Cacheteadas, 100
    Crispy Tacos, 94
    Easy al Pastor Tacos, 92
    Tacos de Bistec, 103
    Tacos Gobernador, 99
Tamales, 178–179
T-Bone Steak, 119
temperatures, cooking, 31
Texas Brisket, 184–185
Texas Chicken Halves, 195
Texas Chili Enchiladas, 149
Texas Chili, 160–161
Texas pipe smokers and grills, 21, 21
Texas Pork Ribs, 187
Texas trailer smokers, 21, 21
Tex-Mex Enchiladas, 150–151
thermometers, 31
tomatillos, 27
    Enchiladas Suizas, 146–147
    Fire-Roasted Salsa, 48
    Green Fajita Marinade, 62
    Salsa Puya, 52
    Salsa Verde—Aguacate, 44
    Salsa Verde—Tomatillos, 42
    Tortas de Deshebrada, 96
tomatoes, 27. See also Roma
    tomatoes
    ArnieTex Tejano Burger, 115
    canned, in Salsa Chipotle en
        Adobo, 50
tomato paste
    Carne Guisada, 122–123
    Charro Beans, 202
    Chile Colorado, 140–141
    Pollo Guisado, 155
    Texas Chili, 160–161
tomato sauce
    Arroz con Pollo, 136
    Calabaza con Pollo, 139
    Caldo de Res, 153
    Carne con Papas, 134

Carne Guisada, 122–123
Charro Beans, 202
Fideo, 167
MommaTex's Mexican Rice,
    207
Picadillo, 144
tools
    barbecue, 16, 18–19
    kitchen, 17
Tortas de Deshebrada, 96
tortillas. See also corn tortillas;
    flour tortillas
    Con Huevos–Papas, 68
    Discada Norteña, 158
    Smoked Barbacoa, 169
Tostadas (aka Chalupas), 133
Totopos
    Botana (RGV Style), 126
    recipe, 211
tumbleweeds, 22, 22
turkey breast, in Smoked Turkey
    Breast, 190

vermicelli noodles, in Fideo, 167

## W-X-Y-Z

Wagyu cows, 31
weather, cook times and, 31
whole chicken
    Caldo de Pollo, 135
    Texas Chicken Halves, 195
wood chips, 22, 23
    Beef Ribs (Loaded Ribs), 199
    Mollejas, 173
    Smoked Barbacoa, 169
    Steak (Porterhouse or T-Bone),
        119
    Steak (Rib Eye), 121
    Texas Pork Ribs, 187
wood chunks, 22, 23
    Beef Ribs (Loaded Ribs), 199
    Mollejas, 173
    Pork Belly Chicharrón, 188–189
    Smoked Barbacoa, 169
    Steak (Porterhouse or T-Bone),
        119
    Steak (Rib Eye), 121
    Texas Pork Ribs, 187
wood species, 23
Worcestershire sauce
    ArnieTex Tejano Burger, 115
    Beef Ribs (Monster Ribs), 198
    Hamburgesa Mexicana, 116
    Texas Chili, 160–161
    Tortas de Deshebrada, 96

## ABOUT THE AUTHOR

**ARNIE "ARNIETEX" SEGOVIA** is a barbecue lover from Texas. A former barbecue competitor, he was one of the first inductees into the International Barbeque Cookers Association Hall of Fame—a spot he earned after hundreds of wins (and walks) on the cook-off trail and for his contributions to the sport in Texas.

During his 20-year cook-off career, he also hosted numerous backyard and competition classes around the state, teaching hundreds of fellow barbecue enthusiasts how to cook great food at home and jump-start their own cook-off journeys. This led him to create the Pitmaster Class, an online community of more than 3,000 members who all share the same mission: to cook great-tasting food and create lasting memories through their cooking.

Today you'll find Arnie on social media as "ArnieTex," sharing his love of barbecue, carne asada, comida casera, and family recipes with his worldwide audience of millions of followers and subscribers. His goal is still the same: to share his love of cooking and the traditions that come with it, all while creating amazing memories with friends and family.